# RQ
## *Relationship Intelligence*

*Why Your RQ*
*Is More Important*
*To Your Success*
*And Happiness*
*Than Your IQ*

Richard A. Panzer

Center for Educational Media

*Relationship Intelligence: why your RQ is more important to your health and happiness than your IQ*

Published by the
Center for Educational Media
P.O. Box 97, Westwood, NJ 07675
800-221-6116/ CenEdMedia@aol.com
www.lovesmarts.com

Design and Layout: Rod Cameron

Cartoon illustrations by Mark Moore from *Angels Bar & Grill* comic published by the Center for Educational Media.

Charts adapted from the *After the Sexual Revolution: the role of marriage in society* multimedia presentation published by the Center for Educational Media.

Photograph on page 13 by permission of Larry Nichols, on page 14 by permission of Lakita Garth

Printed by Hignell Printing Ltd., Winnipeg, MB. Canada
ISBN 1-888933-11-9

## Take the "Love Smarts" test and find out if your RQ is post-grad or pre-K!

• Why are people who fall in love "on drugs"? Why do they need to be careful about becoming "romance junkies"?

• What are the four stages of intimacy and why do many people never get beyond stage two?

• Is "living together" a good way to find if someone is a good marriage partner?

• Which surprising group has the best sex, health, and longest life expectancy?

• Why do "good girl/bad girl" stereotypes persist throughout the world?

• Why do declining rates of marriage endanger the physical safety of women and children as well as men?

• How is youth violence linked to their parents' sexuality?

• Which popular 20th century beliefs about sexuality are based on junk science and why do they hurt men, women and children?

• How can you avoid falling into the "Fairy Tale," "Love conquers all," "Entitlement," "Virtual Reality," "Lone Ranger" and other relationship traps?

• What group is the most endangered species in TV-land?

• Why were many men happy to become "feminists"?

• Why do most college courses on marriage and family flunk the *Relationship Intelligence* test?

• What are the trends that could make the 21st century an age of *Relationship Intelligence?*

### *To find out your score, keep reading!*

# preface

Even though I have been talking about Sexuality and Relationships for 10 years, I still feel like an innocent child asking questions which can never really be answered. The realities of sexual diseases such as AIDS and human papilloma virus are more or less clear, if sobering. The human desire for intimacy is where things get complicated.

When Cupid shoots his love-potion tipped arrows, the rational part of our brains goes into a deep sleep. As the object of our affections enters our consciousness, part of us wants to melt into a malleable gelatin ready to take on any form requested. Experience leads most of us to realize that following this romantic streak must be carefully thought out, lest it end in disaster instead of some approximation of paradise.

I recently heard the tragic story of a bright, energetic young woman living in Columbus, Ohio. She did very well in her studies in high school and was accepted at an Ivy League school on an athletic scholarship. She was the first one in her family and one of the few in her neighborhood able to go to college. The college's health exam revealed that she was HIV-positive. She'd had sex with just one person, a young man she'd known most of her life.

I thought about this young woman, her anguish and her regret. Thousands of girls like her in high school or college have sexual intercourse without the same consequences. Many do end up pregnant. Many get other diseases which are more widespread and, usually, less lethal than AIDS. They get more time to learn from, or at least survive, their mistakes. Despite advances in the medical treatment of HIV/AIDS, she is unlikely to get the same chance.

Some would argue that sexually transmitted diseases are just dumb germs who don't care who you are and whether this is your first or tenth partner. And they're right.

While it's true this young woman made her own decisions and must live with the consequences, I can't stop thinking that the way our society understands and discusses love and sexuality is a travesty. On the one side are those who think that everything can be solved by leaving boxes of condoms around everywhere, as actress Sharon Stone suggested at World's AIDS Day in 1998. On the other side are those who think that just telling young people to just "say no" is enough.

Beyond advice, warnings or commandments regarding sexual expression, there are larger issues-what is the connection between love and sexuality? The 20th century saw a radical departure from the mainstream of traditional wisdom about this important area of our lives. As we enter the 21st century should we build on 20th century trends? Should we junk our recent past as a failure and start from scratch?

An article in *Parade* magazine mentioned the upcoming 55th wedding anniversary of actor Charlton Heston and his wife, Lydia. Asked if she ever considered divorcing the *Ben-Hur* star, Mrs. Heston replied, "Divorce? Never! Murder, yes."

As a child of divorced parents, I didn't see "up close and personal" the strength and security expressed in her kidding response. I've met other couples from the same World War II generation who have the same unquestioning commitment to each other. It's hard not to have enormous respect and even awe at their beautiful faith in their marital relationship. Who wouldn't love to have that kind of respect and friendship after 50 years of being together?

More recent generations are a different story. Last year for a TV show pilot I interviewed couples at a local mall regarding many of these questions about love and relationships. Many couples were insightful. Some were confused. All seemed to be still searching as if there is no clearly successful model to emulate. When asked about the best way to prepare for marriage, many thought that "living together" was a good idea, even though there's a lot of research showing that living together usually damages the chances of a marriage lasting.

Some people will ask why a book about relationships spends so much time focusing on sexual issues. The reason is that the way we deal with sex impacts not only the man-woman relationship itself and any children born as a consequence of intercourse, but also the way we relate to others and, most of all, to ourselves. Sexuality is powerful and its distortion can have consequences on our own lives and those of others for generations to come. Of course, in the right context it's great!

As we go to press, a friend has just emailed me a quote from Sharon Stone (mentioned earlier) about her marriage to Phil Bronstein: "I had no idea what marriage could be. Married, loving sex? I don't care how much you might be in love with someone, there's nothing like married, loving sex. There is no way to tell someone who hasn't had that experience what it does to the way you look at the world." (Sept. 1999 *Movieline)* If Ms. Basic Instinct can have a change of heart, there must be hope for the rest of us . .

If there *is* hope we had better bottle it as quickly as possible and give it out to our kids by the truckloads. A PBS Frontline documentary, "The Lost Children of Rockdale County," which first aired in October, 1999 painted a painful picture of rootless teens disconnected from parents who were themselves confused. One of the girls, Brandi, shares a sentiment, echoed by many of the girls, that sex no longer means intimacy with someone who cares, it's something you do because you're bored:

*"I mean the first time that you have sex you think it's cause it means somethin'. But then you realize it doesn't. You just don't really care anymore...God I know I should, you know, have more feelings, be more soft-hearted and not so cold-hearted about especially when it comes to sex. Not be so just lettin' it be a thing to me."*

This book will attempt to make sense of the confusion expressed by Brandi's generation and to summarize the research of many bright and thoughtful people. I would like to acknowledge my indebtedness to: the *Medical Institute for Sexual Health,* the *National Fatherhood Initiative,* the *Coalition for Marriage, Family and Couples Education,* the *Institute for American Values*, Patrick Fagan at the *Heritage Foundation,* Richard Stedman, Dr. Les and Leslie Parrott, the writings of economist George Gilder, Michael Medved's analysis of mass media, Judith Wallerstein's reexamination of the long-term effects of divorce, Dr. Linda Waite's research on cohabitation at the University of Chicago, psychologist Harville Hendrix, marital therapist Pat Love, as well as social historians Barbara Dafoe Whitehead, David Popenoe, David Blankenhorn, Don Browning, Maggie Gallagher, Wendy Shalit and many others.

I'd also like to thank my good friend John Williams who has pointed me in fruitful directions, Rod Cameron for his artistry on many projects we've worked on, June Saunders for her painstaking proofreading and editing of the text, Michael Balcomb, Kerry Pobanz, Dr. Nancy Victory and my father, Stewart Panzer, M.D. for their helpful suggestions and most of all my wife, Miho, for her support for this and other dreams-in-development.

Richard A. Panzer, Author

# CONTENTS

# CONTENTS

# Introduction

## Why buy the cow if the milk is free?

**First, there was free sex**. Remember all those college types and other enthusiasts of the counterculture who proclaimed that their parents were uptight, particularly about sexual matters? Marriage was just a piece of paper; sex something to be enjoyed with–whomever. Pregnancy was easily avoided with birth control. Remember the laissez faire refrain "if you can't be with the one you love, love the one you're with?"

A generation later, though, we found out that free sex *isn't* free. In fact, it came with a pretty high cost–an epidemic of sexually transmitted diseases (STDs), including a new one–AIDS. Out-of-wedlock pregnancy rates shot through the roof, rising more than 500%. More than a million children are born each year without fathers. AWOL dads are linked to every major social problem, including higher incidences of infant mortality, domestic violence, poverty, juvenile crime, violent crime, poor performance in school.

As years passed, we increasingly heard from the "sexually liberated" not about the joys of a world without rules, but of the emotional costs of uncommitted free sex. A former sorority social director at Indiana University says, "I was pretty bitter toward men my senior year. I didn't trust any of them."

In a Dear Abby letter, a "20 something" woman tells of her passionate one-week fling with a good-looking man at a vacation resort. Two months later, after finding out that she was pregnant, she found out that Mr. Good-looking had no interest in talking with her and hung up before she was able to tell him that she is carrying his child.

If forbidden fruits are no longer forbidden for adults, the teen and even preteen market can't be far behind. But in a society which worships youth, many of the young already feel old: a girl in the ninth grade who had sex with many boys the year before said, "I already feel so old."

In a rare moment of candor, a teenage boy confesses "After four weeks of having sex as often as I wanted, I was tired of her. I didn't see any point in continuing the relationship. I finally left her, which made me feel even worse, because I could see she was hurting."

The emotional costs of "casual," short-term sexual relationships hit sexually active teenage girls hard. They have a six times higher likelihood to attempt suicide than girls who haven't had sex. But even without attempted suicide, "free sex" has left a legacy of worry and anxiety. Teens who used to worry about who likes whom now worry "Do I have AIDS?" or "What do I do now that she's pregnant?" Then there is the guilt about using someone you didn't really care that much about, the pain of damaged relationships, the inability to trust. This is freedom?

Many wonder, like the Sheryl Crowe song says, "If it makes

> # "IF IT MAKES YOU HAPPY,
> ## then it can't be bad;
> ## IF IT MAKES YOU HAPPY,
> ## THEN WHY DO YOU LOOK
> ## SO DAMN SAD?"           :-(

you feel happy, then it can't be bad; if it makes you feel happy, then why do you look so damn sad?"

We learned that sex makes you feel good, but it can kill you, or make you sterile. We hear that to be happy you need to be sexy. Yet, if only losers and nerds are missing out on the fun, why do so many sexually active girls try to take their own lives?

With the advent of AIDS in the '80s and '90s, free sex was replaced with "Safe Sex." Government-sponsored TV ads, Magic Johnson and rap groups alike warned us to remember our "rubbers." High school health teachers lectured on the need to practice "safe(r) sex," and school nurses gave out mint-flavored and no-flavored condoms, depending on whether one wanted oral sex or genital intercourse.

But then we found out that "safe sex" wasn't all that safe. A National Institute of Health study of the effectiveness of condoms in preventing the spread of the AIDS virus in San Fransisco was *canceled* because the study's director says it would be "unethical" to expose so many to the risk of infection, even with condoms.

A leading advocate and practitioner of "safe sex" who was not

infected when he began propagating the "safe sex" message, died from AIDS, in his forties. In Los Angeles, a young AIDS educator who could recite the rules of "safe sex" like a math table became HIV-infected, before the age of 20.

A Johns Hopkins School of Public Health journal reported that among couples in which one partner was already HIV-infected, 1 in 4 of the female sex partners became infected despite using condoms *every time they had sex.*

If free sex isn't free and Safe Sex isn't all that safe, then what's left? A little noticed, but increasing trend towards committed, monogamous relationships is under way in the U.S., what could be called *Relationship Intelligence.*

Relationship Intelligence is a search for intimacy without anxiety or guilt, for freedom within the bounds of real trust and commitment. An attractive "30 something" TV contributor on MSNBC-TV explains, "I used to complain to my mother, who is a liberal, about boyfriends who seemed commitment shy. And she would say, 'Well, why buy the cow, if the milk is free?' We're in the sexual promised land now; the milk is free; people are surfeited with sex.

And yet we're starved for love... I didn't kiss the man I'm dating now, until the seventh date. I didn't have sex with him until the seventh month. He respects and values me a lot more than the men I dated in college, when I was a lot more casual with my body."

A.C. Green

NBA star A.C. Green is in his 30s and a virgin. Green admits that abstaining from extramarital sex is one of the most unpopular things a person can do, and runs against the grain of what red-blooded American males, especially athletes, are supposed to want and do. He says, "it's ironic, but the guys who are parents–and especially the guys who have daughters–tend to look at sex before marriage a lot more carefully now." Isn't it obvious that he's a lot more radical than Dennis Rodman will ever be?

A poll at U.C.L.A. reveals that 40% of undergraduates are virgins. A surprising number of college students are deciding that uncommitted sex is not worth the effort. They'd rather wait.

Brown University's Rajib Chanda, a senior fraternity president who founded a computer dating service, says, "in a normal Brown relationship, you meet, get drunk, hook up and either avoid eye contact the next day or find yourself in a relationship that consists of a headlong plunge into a pool of intimacy when students were really looking just to tip a toe."

Chanda explains about the new trend at Brown. Instead of pairing off, many undergrads socialize in unpartnered packs. They go out to dinner in groups, attend movies in groups, and at parties dance in a circle of five or six. The packs give students a sense of self-assurance and identity but keep them from deeper, more complicated relationships, which Chanda says, "may be just the point."

In Washington, D.C., the singles scene is no longer just bars, dances, or parties. Since 1997 singles can meet while serving at a soup kitchen or building a house for homeless people. Dana Kressierer, co-founder of Single Volunteers of D.C., says, "In our group, the superficiality of singles bars and dances isn't there. People are meeting with no makeup on and up to their knees in mud. You meet in your natural state, so it's about who you are, not what you look like or how much money you make or what kind of car you drive." Kressierer says that even if you don't meet "the one," people often say they've met their 'best friend,' not a bad place to start.

Lakita Garth

In the 1990s, for the first time in 20 years, the proportion of high school students who have had sexual intercourse at least once dropped by 11%. More than half of teens are choosing to wait.

Even the media managed to discover the existence of real-live virgins. *VOGUE* magazine in an article named "Like a Virgin, Again" wondered why "twenty-five years after women began fighting for the right to have–and enjoy–sex, many young women are postponing carnal knowledge."

*Witness Lakita Garth, a born-again, 26 year-old spokesperson for a Los Angeles-based group called Athletes for Abstinence. Her agenda was heavily Christian, but she was no humorless, scrubbed-face zealot. She was a beautiful young African American entertainer who delivered her abstinence rap with impassioned ease...*

*"The girls who laughed at me in high school because I was a virgin," she told me, "are now working at a K mart checkout counter and have two babies by different men. When people say to me, 'You've missed something,' I say, 'Yeah, I missed worrying about being pregnant and getting some STD [sexually transmitted disease] and having some hospital orderly change my diapers because I'm lying in a hospital bed dying of AIDS and having chronic diarrhea.' I want to be able to look my husband in the face on our wedding night," she told me with a beatific smile, "and say, 'I saved myself for you.' "*

VOGUE's writer is shocked to find the idea of premarital chastity taking hold not just among the strongly religious, but even among typical college coeds you'd expect to have a more carefree attitude toward exploring and expressing their sexuality:

*I could see how her moral resolution might work for the committedly religious, but it was hard to imagine her message playing out among college coeds. It made sense that they would be scared of AIDS and other diseases, even alert to pregnancy fears. But what of this idea of "saving" yourself?*

*As I talked with these women I was surprised to discover the degree to which their language and emotions accorded with Garth's vision. They didn't talk about God, but they did talk about love, tenderness, commitment—and about not having sex without it. Most were not strictly virgins. Many had had sex once or twice and then retreated behind a Maginot Line. They are what the promoters of abstinence like to call "secondary virgins," and I ran in to a lot of them, young women who told me how they wished they hadn't done it. They felt dirty, somehow, lonesome, and were determined not to have sex again short of a wedding or engagement ring—or, at the very least, love.*

*"The thing that really bugs me is that I didn't love him," a lovely Asian high school senior told me about the boyfriend she had slept with a few times and had just broken up with. "We weren't doing it every single day, like some of my friends," she continued, looking down at her scuffed saddle shoes, struggling with tears. "I don't feel bad about it, but I think*

*that, actually, maybe I'd wait to be engaged or married the next time. I've had it; I know what it's like; it's no big deal. I'd want something permanent before having sex again, some stability, a reason he won't leave or I won't leave."* A. T. Fleming, "Up Front: like a virgin, again," *VOGUE*

There are even changes in the marriage-hostile world of TV. A 1998 NYPD Blue show concludes with an explicit, steamy sex scene between Detective Di Simone and Detective Diane Rusell. After their passionate groans, she says, "I think we just made a baby." Di Simone sighs, "Great!"

I was ready to write this off as another sexploitation scene when I remembered that Di Simone and Russell *are married.* How many TV shows suggest that married people even know what sex is, much less do it? Doesn't the gospel according to NBC, ABC, and CBS teach that getting married kills your sex drive? After all, a hot, steamy sex scene between a man *and his wife* is light years apart from its meaning in the unmarried state. To witness such a positive affirmation of the value of marriage, the idea of pregnancy *welcomed* and embraced by the NYPD Blue couple left me—speechless. I'd come to the show expecting to be scandalized and ended up. . .well, almost like being in church, well maybe not inside, but at least at the front steps. Not the usual pomp and ceremony, but the same uplifting, *life affirming* message.

Besides these signs of a nascent cultural shift towards secure, committed relationships, there are indicators of a new emerging scientific consensus on sexuality and relationships. Science, which once promised "magic bullet" solutions to pregnancy and sexually transmitted diseases, is less bullish (some would say arrogant) than it once was. Scientific research no longer debunks monogamy and marriage, but converges regularly with what defenders of the traditional family have been saying for decades.

To give an example: the largest, most scientific survey of sex in America ever, conducted at the University of Chicago, found that marital commitment may not just be a moral ideal, *it can be good for your sex life and your health.* The study found that married people had more sex than singles. Nine out of 10 married couples said they were very emotionally and physically satisfied with their sex lives. While unwed couples living together had just as much sex, they were much less emotionally fulfilled in their relationships. Those with more than one sex partner in the last year were the *least* emotionally satisfied. This leads one to wonder–is it possible that Ozzie and Harriet having more fun in the sack than James Bond and Girls X, Y, or Z ever had? If he were dead, Hugh Hefner would turn over in his grave. But he's not dead. He's married again. At least he was until recently. Let's just say he's trying.

What about the Generation Xers, many of whom saw their parents divorce one or even two times? A 1998 *Newsweek* article, "Down the Aisle," reports that these 20-and-30-somethings, though often bereft of role models, are in many ways more conservative than their parents. They are "more likely to value the stability that marriage can provide," and "determined to succeed where their parents failed."

In fact, market-research firm Yankelovich Partners reports that 73% of Gen-Xers said they'd be in favor of a return to more traditional standards in family life. Only 56% of baby boomers felt the same way when asked the same question twenty years ago.

And while these marriage-seekers may lack skills and role models for their marriages, a growing marriage education movement is also rising up to help engaged and newly married couples gain practical insights as to how to make love last.

Beginning in January 1999, the state of Florida began offering discounted marriage licenses to couples who could prove they'd undergone several hours of premarital counseling. In Louisiana and Arizona, laws allow couples to choose "covenant marriages," in which getting divorced would be more difficult and preceded by several months of marriage counseling. Utah has established a "Marriage Commission" which has the explicit purpose of finding ways to strengthen marriage in the state.

Around the country, more than 100 cities and towns have instituted a community marriage policy in which all the churches pledge to require in-depth premarital counseling and education for every couple seeking to marry. Mike McManus, founder of the *Marriage Savers* movement, says that 80% of marriages, even those on the verge of divorce, can be saved.

So while the editors of *Cosmopolitan* and *Penthouse* are unlikely to change their profitable tune, there is evidence of a return in American culture towards marriage. Is this a blip on the screen or a trend that will become more and more dominant in the early decades of the 21st century? It remains to be seen, but now let's take a look at some real life stories of several twenty-somethings who have survived free sex, no longer hold faith in Safe Sex and are groping towards relationships of more lasting value.

# Chapter One

True Confessions

*The following stories are all true, with names and locations changed to protect identities.*

## Frank's Story

Frank is in his late 20s. He grew up in New York City, the son of a college professor and a mother who took care of his three older sisters and him. His parents divorced when he was 5.

Frank and his sisters lived with their mom until he was 7. Then he and his youngest sister, Angela, moved in with his father. They attended a Catholic high school in Queens. After graduating, he took one and a half years off before attending college at the State University of New York in New Paltz, where he majored in History.

Frank worked as a bike messenger through his high school and college years to help fund his education. He is athletic, handsome, and personable.

Frank says he was attracted to girls as early as age 6 or 7. Around age 13, when his buddies were talking about which girl they wanted to "do it" with, he would say he only wanted to have sex if "I'm in love with her." He believed in and hoped for "true love." Frank reminisces,

*When I was 12 or 13, my father's second marriage was breaking up due to an affair he was having with someone else. We moved to an exclusive part of the city where there was high security, a haven from crime, but it was full of divorced families and pornography. My friend was babysitting for a divorced woman and we watched the X-rated movies she had.*

*About two years later, we moved again to a new house in a new neighborhood. My sister, Angela, and I were hopeful for a new start, but within a month my father's lover came over. Angela and I knew what they were doing. That's when my father and I began fighting. I lost all respect for him. We fought over the stupidest things.*

*Another time, my father came home from a trip, came into my room, threw a pornographic magazine on my desk and said, "I found this at the airport and don't need it anymore." I had seen porn before, but this was from my own father. It was like a tidal wave. I was so confused. I lost all my reference points, all my earlier ideals about true love sank to the* bottom of the East river. I began to think about sex all the time.

Angela and I moved back with my mother. The first time I kissed a girl it was such a big thing, I thought I was in love. A few months later I became close to a girl named Melinda. We would often drink alcohol from her parents' liquor cabinet. We started fooling around and within a few weeks we began having intercourse. She was 15; I was 17.

All my emotions and thinking went into that first relationship with Melinda; it was all-consuming.  After a year, all of a sudden, I asked myself, "Why am I with you (Melinda)? There are so many other girls I could be with." We broke up, but I still felt attached. I didn't have any other relationships. Soon we got back together.

One year after I'd broken up with her, Melinda broke up with me. I couldn't function–I felt so much pain. But then she would come around sometimes. I realized it was a game for her, to keep me in her control without committing herself to me. I was like a puppet in her hands. I would probably have done the same thing to her, if I had been in control. It was like a drug; my mind knew the relationship was wrong, but my emotions were too strong.

Finally, I decided to completely break it off. After I did that, I felt I was getting stronger. One day she showed up, just before she was going to California to visit her father. She wanted me to sleep with her. I told her I wasn't interested. For three hours she pleaded with me to come to her house, telling me how much she loved me, that I was the "only one." She said whatever she could to get me to come over. Finally, I gave in.

The next day, I saw her off at the airport. She said she would call, but never did. I felt totally manipulated, the biggest sucker on the planet.

Soon afterwards, I went to college. I never wanted to be in a weak position with girls again. I started to take total control in relationships with girls. I hurt them the same way I had been hurt.

After the first semester of school, I began to go out with Lisa. Our relationship went off and on for about a year. It was totally based on alcohol and sex.

In the middle of my sophomore year, I cut off from all women. For six months, I felt so empty. My mother was involved in encounter groups where people shared about their feelings. One time I went with her to a meeting. For the first time, I could feel and release a lot of pain. I began to become more conscious, see myself more clearly. I began to feel stronger.

There was a girl, Debbie, at school I really respected. I was very attracted to her. Finally, I approached her and we started seeing each other. We didn't have sex until two months later. I was trying to learn *how to love. Our relationship went on for four years.*

*After college, I came back to New York City. She was still in New Paltz. I realized that no matter how good a person Debbie was, there was*

*still something wrong with me, so I broke it off in 1991.*

*I was abstinent for four years until I got engaged to Melanie. Sometimes I struggled to be abstinent, but I realized I had a lot of sex for selfish reasons. For the first time since I became a teenager, I tried to avoid any sexual thoughts–I realized, "you can't control yourself." It became a challenge to me. Either I would gain mastery over it or never be able to have control of my life.*

*I thought about my ideals of true love before porn came into my life. I realized that unless I have deep, unselfish love for Melanie, selfishness would corrupt our sexual relationship. We're not having sex until we get married. I feel more free to develop our relationship in other ways.*

*Melanie is a virgin. I want to achieve a real victory over sexual thoughts–I want to experience true love with her, have children someday.*

# Beverly's Story

Beverly, a petite 23 year-old actress with light brown hair and a ready smile, grew up in a suburb of Louisville, Kentucky. Her father was a self-employed graphics artist. Her mother helped with her husband's business and took care of the family and home.

Ever since she was 11 years old Beverly's been involved in the theater–either community theater, the high school drama club, or at college. During the summer after her freshman year, she worked as an intern with a traveling theater group.

Beverly says,

*My father is a saint, goodhearted and loving. My mother is a manic-depressive who blames all her problems on her own father and on my dad. My dad says he loves my mom, but it's obviously a difficult situation.*

*Even in kindergarten, elementary and middle schools, I had boyfriends. I would "go steady" for a week and then break up. My first real date was when I was 13. Through high school, I was just dating, nothing steady. Often I would flirt with someone who already had a girlfriend.*

*My first real serious relationship was when I was a senior in high school. Ron was a year younger than I. Our relationship lasted for 3-4 months and then he split without saying goodbye to go follow the Grateful Dead. Then he showed up two months later.*

*I was involved with one of his friends. I was so infatuated with Ron that I dumped his friend, who was such a good and kind person, in order to go back to Ron.*

*After I went back to college, we continued our relationship by long distance. He broke up with me on Thanksgiving. Later on, around Valentine's Day, he visited me again. I couldn't reject Ron–I liked him too much.*

*My first time to have sex was when I was 17. It was the November before I met Ron. It was a guy I worked with at a pub whom I barely knew. He asked me if I wanted to go to a party, so I said OK. It was while I was driving us in my car that I found out there was no party.*

*He asked me to pull over, so I did. He started to make advances. I couldn't think of any reason to stop him, so we did it. My girlfriends were having sex. My parents never said anything one way or another about it, so there was no reason not to. I didn't feel anything. It was my last day of work, so I never saw him again. I felt nothing.*

Later when I started going out with Ron, he introduced me to marijuana and LSD. Within a month we started having sex, almost every other day at his place, since both of his parents were working. Sometimes we did it in the woods, since he was into nature.

I soon realized that at the same time Ron was seeing me, he also had two other girlfriends. I was obsessed with him. He had a lot of abilities. He was a drummer and good at sports. He was the center of attention

wherever he went, very charismatic and powerful. I became just like him, a "Dead" follower. I dressed in the same style with the round John Lennon glasses, sandals, beads, and long skirts.

Later, in college, after Ron and I'd broken up, I met Ben, who was a junior and four years older than I. Ben was similar to Ron, only more brilliant. Girls were crazy about him. He was also the center of attention, an artist who could draw really well and a rap artist, even though he was white.

I began to dress hiphop with the ski hats and really baggy clothes, just like Ben. I was totally infatuated with him. He would spend a night with me every three or four weeks. I would live for that one night. He was having relationships with other girls, especially his old girlfriend, who was black. She was very beautiful, a model. They broke up, probably because he couldn't be faithful.

**H**e treated me more like a friend with whom he was sometimes intimate. I strategized how to become the closest of anyone to him, and I succeeded. I would hang around on campus just in case he would walk by. Many people thought we were boyfriend and girlfriend, but not him.

When I left for the summer theater internship, I felt satisfied that I was impressing Ben. The theater director, Mike, was brilliant. Since I was the first summer intern the theater group had ever had, he was totally dedicated to teaching me. He was 31. It was so exciting to be the recipient of someone who was so creative.

He wasn't sleeping with the women involved in the theater group, even though he probably could have. He was so focused. He didn't go to parties. I learned so much about art and performance. We started to sleep together, but it was a secret, just like with Ron and Ben.

In my sophomore year, Ben and I lived next door to each other. I was inspired by my summer internship to start my own theater group. Almost every night I would sleep over but we wouldn't have sex, just once every few weeks. I was disappointed; it was like getting crumbs off a table.

After doing it, the next day I would ask him, "Are we a couple?" He would always say, "no." Then I would ask, "then why did we do it last night? You said we weren't going to." Then he would say "OK, no more." But then we'd do it in a few weeks. I couldn't resist him, better to have a little than to have nothing. He was on my mind constantly.

It went on this way the whole sophomore year. In the summer, I went to see Mike and the theater group again and then I got a job.

I began to realize that none of these three men I've been involved with, Ron, Ben, and Mike, were committed to me. I was always an occasional mistress, a secret, an afterthought. In addition, I had seven or eight one night stands. Even though I didn't really want those one night stands I couldn't think of any reason not to. I felt it would have been mean to stop when we had already gone so far, after the guy was already stimulated. At the end of my sophomore year, I finally decided that I would never be intimate with someone I didn't care about.

During that year, I was living in what was the party center of the campus. People would often get drunk, even have sex in our living room. Around Valentine's Day, I began to have anxiety attacks. It lasted for two weeks. I couldn't eat. I felt so secluded, alone. School counselors couldn't help. I had to leave that sickening environment. I was just surviving. I kept trying to find a source of inspiration.

I started to look to my father. My father is very religious, close to God. He doesn't attend church, but he reads the Bible often and prays. So when I was getting an anxiety attack, I would pray. I began to feel relieved; more normal; centered.

I met a spiritual group where I felt at home. I was shocked to find that the men and women who weren't married didn't have sex. The guys weren't nerds; many of them were good-looking, but they weren't doing it. I looked in the Bible and in other religious books. They all said the same thing: don't have any sex unless you are married.

My parents had never told me not to. My father, even though he was religious, didn't bring it up. My mother was never happy with any of my friends, girls or guys, so I never felt that she particularly cared about this issue.

Looking back, I realized that I had sex because I wanted to be loved and thought that was the way to attract the men I wanted to love me. I began to understand how little I was settling for, how little value I was giving myself. This only became clear after I separated from that lifestyle. Then it hit me like a ton of bricks.

I've been abstinent for five years. Giving up the sex wasn't very hard, though sometimes I missed the emotional involvement. But I understood how terrible was my taste in men. Like my mother, I was looking for a man to fill all my emotional needs. Like her, when they disappointed me, I blamed them, even though I was willing to be used by them and tried to manipulate them in various ways. I began to see that I need to be spiritually and emotionally whole myself before I will truly be able to love a man.

Now I'm engaged to Alan. He's totally different from my old boyfriends. He's very shy, even awkward. He's kind and thoughtful. Several women in the theater used to tell me, "Don't go for the popular guys. Go for the nerd, he'll stay with you." Alan is not a nerd, but he is definitely more unselfish, more down-to-earth, less self-centered.

Love comes from commitment, not from chemicals, attractions, and sparks. Infatuation no longer interests me. I am focusing on developing myself, not just as an extension of a man. Being attractive to men or enticing them with some parts of me, is no longer a source of happiness to me. I want my whole being to be accepted.

**"To us, sex is special,"** says a 20-something couple who want to wait.

► Nicole, 23, and Rod, 26, met through a church Youth Group and began dating soon after. Nicole works with mentally retarded people. Rod is a payroll manager.

"Self-respect is a large part of my decision not to have premarital sex," explains Nicole. "I've seen the respect a male loses for a female once she has satisfied him sexually and I've seen men cheat on women who have given them everything. I decided when I was 21 that the only way to safeguard myself against being hurt in that way was not to have sex before marriage.

"I've had two boyfriends before Rodney and we broke up because of my views on premarital sex. If a guy dumps me just because I won't have sex with him, *then he doesn't deserve me.* It's easy to feel pressured into having sex by partners or peers. One schoolfriend always acted as if my not having sex was 'uncool', but it isn't that I'm a prude–I just want to wait until the time is right. I see sex as being too special to waste on just anyone.

"When I started going out with Rod, we knew sex wouldn't be part of the equation because we are both committed to our faith. It's a constant struggle, but we make it easier by avoiding certain situations. We won't go away or spend a night together. We hold hands and hug and if there's an intimate touch that excites us, we'll avoid doing it again. I think because we've waited, when we do make love, it will be a very spiritual and emotional experience for both of us."

"When I was in my late teens," says Rod, " I knew people in sexual relationships who were getting hurt, so I thought there must be something in what the church was saying about saving sex. I wanted to be able to make a rational decision about who I had a relationship with, and the easiest way to do that, without getting hurt, was to take sex out of the picture and not let the fact that I might have slept with someone cloud my judgment.

"I've seen how quickly a guy loses interest in a woman who has been around and I have a lot of respect for Nicole because I know the choice she has made is a tough one. I've been in short-term relationships where sex has been expected of me, and it's been a complete turn-off for some women when I haven't come up with the goods. People assume you're a bit strange or don't like sex. But I do have feelings, I just keep them under control. And I think there is more trust in our relationship because of that. Sex is on the back burner, so Nicole understands that if that was all I was interested in, I'd have left by now. We have romance without the passion. I buy her flowers or a gift or write her letters - just being in each other's company satisfies us. To me, sex is special, but if you're having it with every Tom, Dick or Harry, then it isn't special anymore—it's sport."

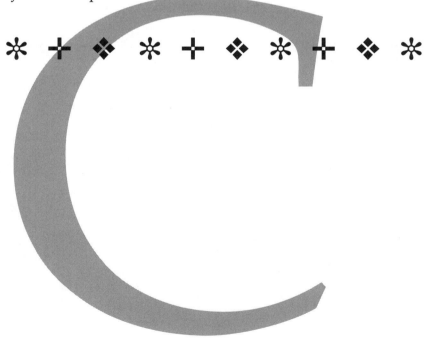

✳ ✚ ❖ ✳ ✚ ❖ ✳ ✚ ❖ ✳

# Chapter Two

## stages of
## *Intimacy*

Attraction,
Infatuation, Connection,
and Caretaking

Young love is a flame; very pretty, very hot and fierce, but still only light and flickering. The love of the older and disciplined heart is as coals, deepburning , unquenchable.

Henry Ward Beecher

"Romantic love is supposed to end.  It is nature's glue, which brings two incompatible people together for the purpose of mutual growth. When romantic love dies, it clears the way for real love. The creation of real love is nature's way of repairing and completing itself–through you."[1]

Harville Hendrix, Author and Marriage Counselor

*I can remember stories, those things my mother said.*
*She told me fairy tales, before I went to bed.*
*She spoke of happy endings, then tucked me in real tight.*
*She turned my night light on, and kissed my face good night.*
*My mind would fill with visions, of perfect paradise.*

*She told me everything, she said he'd be so nice.*
*He'd ride up on his horse and, take me away one night.*
*I'd be so happy with him, we'd ride clean out of sight.*
*She never said that we would, curse, cry and scream and lie.*
*She never said that maybe, someday he'd say goodbye.*

*She spoke about happy endings, of stories not like this.*
*She said he'd slay all dragons, defeat the evil prince.*
*She said he'd come to save me, swim through the stormy seas.*
*I'd understand the story, it would be good for me.*

*You never came to save me, you let me stand alone.*
*Out in the wilderness, alone in the cold.*

*You never came to save me, you let me stand alone.*
*Out in the wilderness, alone in the cold.*
*I found no magic potion, no horse with wings to fly.*
*I found the poison apple, my destiny to die.*

> *No royal kiss could save me, no magic spell to spin.*
> *My fantasy is over, my life must now begin.*
>
> *My story ends, as stories do.*
> *Reality steps into view.*
> *No longer living life in paradise-or fairy tales-*
>
> **Selection from *Fairy Tales:* Anita Baker**, Vernon Fails
> and Michael Powell

# Why Sex?

Have you ever asked yourself, "why sex?" Yes, of course, it is through sex that we, along with most of the animal and plant world, reproduce. There are seemingly easier ways. Parthenogenesis–virgin birth–the mode of procreation favored by amoebas and stick insects, would be more simple.

New biological research suggests that sex is essential for our survival; it functions like a broom to sweep away bad mutations that would otherwise drag us quickly into deadly obsolescence. Two British biologists have estimated that on average 2-3 bad mutations have occurred for each person in history. This is an amazing number when one realizes that a mutation can only disappear when its owner, or child or grandchild, dies without offspring.

If we bred like stick insects, the children would have the exact same faults as their parents. The next generation would have those faults plus any new bad mutations. Bad mutations would accumulate with potentially negative or even deadly birth defects.

Sex operates like one of life's largest non-regulated lotteries. One's genes, all of which exist in pairs with one being dominant and the other recessive, first get shuffled among themselves to produce the "half deck" of genes of a particular egg or sperm. A random assortment is then cut into someone else's half deck (when the genes in a particular sperm merge with the genes of a particular egg). Bad mutations either get left behind on the cutting floor in the first shuffling of the deck, or are matched with a more dominant "healthier" gene. If bad genes from both parents combine in a fetus, their synergistic effect will probably cause a speedy death, eliminating many mutations at once.

In this sense, biologists say, the gamble of sex beats death. By not acting like stick insects, we escape extinction.[2] The only time this sexual "gene lottery" doesn't work this way, is when two much interbreeding takes place. This happened centuries ago when inbreeding among relatives within the Spanish royal family led to high rates of hemophilia. This may be one reason why there are such strong taboos in most cultures against incest, having sexual intercourse with a close relative.

But let's take a less cold, more romantic, look at the man/woman relationship and the stages of intimacy.

## The First Stage of Intimacy

Attraction towards someone of the opposite sex is a beautiful part of life, a fulfillment of our sexual being. But for something that is so natural, it's amazing how much confusion exists about what it means to love and to be loved. Why, as the song describes, does love so often lead to a multitude of broken dreams and heartaches?

A major reason is the misunderstanding of the stages of intimacy. Pat Love is a family therapist from Austin, Texas[3] who gave a keynote speech at the second annual *Smart Marriages* conference held in Washington, D.C. in the summer of 1998. Many found that her explanation about stages of love and intimacy clarified many issues that all of us struggle with.

First, Dr. Love says, there is the stage of **attraction** to someone, often based upon how that person looks or acts. Someone's personality, mannerisms, or voice may remind you of a relative, or a parent who was very significant to you, even though you may not be conscious at all of the resemblance. Components of attraction include physical appearance expressing health, strength, and fertility, personality qualities such as sense of humor and various kinds of intelligence, psychological issues including unfinished business from childhood, social status, emotional chemistry, and actual chemistry involving DNA and pheromones.

Pheromones are chemicals emitted by individuals to attract other members in the same species. Female moths produce sex pheromones to attract male moths for mating. In the animal world, pheromones exhibit powerful control of sexual behavior. For instance, when an ovulating female boar is exposed to a pheromone from a male boar's saliva, for example, she immediately freezes into a mating posture.[4]

While human sexual attraction is more complex, scientific research is showing that pheromones play a role for us humans as well. One study at the University of Bern, in Switzerland, found that women were most attracted to the t-shirts of men whose genetic makeup was most opposite to their own. This attraction to someone whose genes are different or opposite to our own may have been advantageous in weeding out the "bad mutations," avoiding the inbreeding mentioned above and diversifying the gene pool. Whatever the neurochemical reasons, biological attraction, being as nondiscriminating as it is, it's important to realize that *you can be attracted to a real jerk or jerkette.*

In the second stage of intimacy, called **infatuation**, you are more than just attracted. You are obsessed. Thoughts of that person fill your mind *every waking moment.* You want to spend as much time as possible with your "beloved"! You can't stop thinking of him or her. You feel like you're on top of "cloud nine" when he or she is around, in the pits of hell when separated. You feel like you've always known this person and can't imagine living apart.

In this stage, whether you realize or not, you're on drugs. Not the illegal kind, but drugs that your own body produces. A hormone called oxytocin is produced by a part of the brain called the hypothalamus. Scientists believe that oxytocin strengthens the brain's receptors that produce emotions. You also experience a natural amphetamine-like drug called PEA, phenylethylamine, sometimes called the "love drug," as well as two other natural mood-affecting substances–dopamine and norepinephrine.[5] Since you are on internally created "speed" you feel energized–like you could stay up all night. You feel strong sexual desire because of increased testosterone levels (true for both men and women).

When people are in this stage, it's easy for them to think they're in love. So strong are the feelings that they feel there's no good reason to hold anything back. Many teens and adults go ahead with intimate relations in this stage.

The problem is that when you're infatuated, you don't necessarily have a realistic view of this other person. You think he or she's "da bomb!"–perfect or at least with so many fine qualities the defects don't matter. If someone says, "Maybe you should slow down," you protest: "Why are you being such a party-pooper? I've never been this happy! Why are you trying to take this happiness away from me?"

When someone is using drugs or alcohol, how good is his/her judgment? That person feels all-powerful, with no limits at all. But is that person really all-powerful? No, and the same thing is true about someone who is infatuated. That person can feel grateful for being so happy and connected to another person, but he or she should realize that his/her judgment may not be the best.

Questions to think about when you're infatuated:

---

*1) Even though this person seems to be so cool, so wonderful, how much do I really know about him/her? What kind of relationship does this person have with his family? This tells you a lot about someone. What do people you respect know about this person?*

*2) How does this person treat others, including members of his/her family? With respect or with contempt or bullying? Does this person try to force his/her will on me? (These are signs of abusive behavior and personality.)*

*3) How does this person relate to him/herself? Does she always see herself as a victim? Is he always blaming others?*

*4) How does this person deal with money? Is he an impulsive spender? Does she like to save for the future?*

*5) Does he keep his promises? Does she know how to apologize when she's made a mistake?*

*6) What are this person's values? What does he care about the most? Whom does she admire-who are her heroes? Does this coincide with your own most important values?*

*7) What are his strong points? Weak points? Could you see yourself living with these qualities for the rest of your life? (Many people **wrongly** assume they can change another person's weak points.)*

---

You probably know people who were infatuated. They thought they were in love with someone only to see it fall apart, realizing the other person wasn't really committed to them. The cold slap of reality dashes their dreams to pieces. If they've avoided sex, they feel a sense of relief at having avoided squandering love on someone who didn't deserve it. If they've had sex, they often feel the pain and regret at having given a deep part of themselves to someone who wasn't true.

Having an intimate relationship involving sex may provide relief from feelings of loneliness that we all have, for a while. Sex can mimic feelings of love, but underlying issues of depression or poor relationships aren't solved by having sex. In the end, it often makes things worse.

A study published in the respected journal, *Pediatrics,* found that teen sex is linked to a lot of self-destructive behaviors. Teen guys and girls between the ages of 12 -16 who were sexually active were much more likely to use alcohol, cigarettes, marijuana and other drugs, run away from home, be arrested by the police, or be suspended from school. Teen girls who have lost their virginity

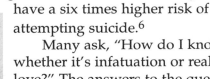

have a six times higher risk of attempting suicide.[6]

Many ask, "How do I know whether it's infatuation or real love?" The answers to the questions above may give you some clues, but the fact is, even if your boyfriend or girlfriend seems to pass all these tests, you still cannot act on the assumption that it's more than a passing infatuation. Whether it develops into something deeper and longer-lasting *cannot* be foreseen at this point.

Would someone who truly cares about you ever ask you to do something that neither of you are ready to take responsibility for, such as creating a new life? It's hard to see how uncommitted sex could be an act of "love" because it's based on a false promise of love without the commitment. Isn't it like saying, "We'll act like we're married even though we're not?"

This contradiction was shown, tragically, in the case of college students Amy Grossberg and her boyfriend Brian Peterson, both of whom were convicted of crimes relating to the death of their newborn son. The baby was found in a dumpster near a Delaware motel soon after its birth. They both acted on the belief that they were grown-up enough to have sex, but the reality of a child born at "the wrong time" was too much for them to take. They took action to "get rid of the problem" by killing their son. Sex is a life-uniting, life-creating act. It is much more significant than many people take it to be.

# The Third Stage of Intimacy-Connection

Selection from *The Velveteen Rabbit* by Margery Williams about a conversation between a toy rabbit and an older toy called the Skin Horse:

*The Skin Horse had lived longer in the nursery than any of the others. He was so old that his brown coat was bald in patches and showed the seams underneath, and most of the hairs in his tail had been pulled out to string bead necklaces. He was wise, for he had seen a long succession of mechanical toys arrive to boast and swagger, and by-and-by break their mainsprings and pass away, and he knew that they were only toys, and would never turn into anything else. For nursery magic is very strange and wonderful, and only those playthings that are old and wise and experienced like the Skin Horse understand all about it.*

*"What is REAL?" asked the Rabbit one day, when they were lying side by side near the nursery fender, before Nana came to tidy the room. "Does it mean having things that buzz inside you and a stick-out handle?"*

*"Real isn't how you are made," said the Skin Horse. "It's a thing that happens to you. When a child loves you for a long, long time, not just to play with, but REALLY loves you, then you become Real."*

*"Does it hurt?" asked the Rabbit.*

*"Sometimes," said the Skin Horse, for he was always truthful. "When you are Real you don't mind being hurt."*

*"Does it happen all at once, like being wound up," he asked, "or bit by bit?"*

*"It doesn't happen all at once," said the Skin Horse. "You become. It takes a long time. That's why it doesn't often happen to people who break easily, or have sharp edges, or who have to be carefully kept. Generally, by the time you are Real, most of your hair has been loved off, and your eyes drop out and you get loose in the joints and very shabby. But these things don't matter at all, because once you are Real you can't be ugly, except to people who don't understand."*

*"I suppose you are Real?" said the Rabbit. And then he wished he had not said it, for he thought the Skin Horse might be sensitive. But the Skin Horse only smiled.*

*"The Boy's Uncle made me Real," he said. "That was a great many*

*years ago; but once you are Real you can't become unreal again. It lasts for always."*

*The Rabbit sighed. He thought it would be a long time before this magic called Real happened to him. He longed to become Real, to know what it felt like; and yet the idea of growing shabby and losing his eyes and whiskers was rather sad. He wished that he could become it without these uncomfortable things happening to him.[7]*

In this childhood story, the Skin Horse says that when some-one really loves you for a long, long time (not just to play with, but really loves you) then you become real. We seek to experience real love from someone who isn't changeable or just for a short time because deep down we all know that lasting love is an essential ingredient in becoming fully human. After all, when your life has run its course, who wants to look back at how much money you made or even how important or famous you became? Isn't the love you gave, the love you shared, one of the key ways you will judge your own life?

The Rabbit wants to become Real, to know what it feels like to be loved, but he is afraid of having his plastic eyes and whiskers fall out. Similarly, while we all seek out love, we often fear its demands, knowing that when you love someone, there are costs–financial, emotional, sacrifices of time and freedom.

Feelings of infatuation must end. In his statement at the beginning of the chapter, Harville Hendrix, the psychologist, explains that infatuation is nature's trick, a Shakespearean *A Mid-Summer Night's Dream*, to bring two incompatible people together for the purpose of mutual growth. No couple can afford to stay in this dreamlike, drug-induced state forever. After being together for months or years after the first moments of infat-uation, it's usual for feelings of neutrality for one's partner to set in. The brain becomes used to the chemical "high" produced by the mix of dopamine, norepinephrine, and PEA and needs greater and greater doses to get the same "buzz."

Other demanding tasks press in that demand clear minds and strong wills. As if afraid to face the future, many couples break up. When the intense feelings wear off, they wonder what they ever saw in their boyfriend/girlfriend and try to find some one else, as if they were "romance junkies" literally addicted to feelings of love. They try to find a new partner to stimulate those PEA "love drug" feelings again and again.

Such people often find it difficult to enter the third stage of intimacy, what Pat Love calls **"Connection."** The relationship is in transition from passion to companionship and a more lasting love: from irrational need and obsession to mutual affirmation and acceptance. Ongoing physical contact, not just sexual excitement, leads the brain to release continued high doses of oxytocin and increased levels of morphinelike substances, endorphins, that lead to feelings of calmness, security, a general sense of wellbeing.[8] In this stage one can feel the joy of *clear-sighted* unity. This deep kind of friendship depends less on passion and more on stability.

Tender looks are the pieces of treasure at this stage. As Peter Ustinov once said, "Love is an act of endless forgiveness, a tender look which becomes a habit." We all enjoy being passionately desired, but even more fulfilling is to be deeply accepted. For your "soulmate" to accept you when he or she knows most, or even all, of your weak points and sees you at your worst, is to experience a deeper level of love.

Lucy says about her twenty-one-year-long love and marriage to Rick: "It becomes so comfortable, you know, like an old shoe." Rick just smiles and says thank you at being compared to an old shoe. Lucy continues, "It's just not that crazy feeling anymore. There's security and caring and it just gets better and better. So the infatuation is gone? You just bring it to another level."[9]

In this stage the character of the other person becomes a very important issue. Whether that person has good or poor qualities of character can lead to your enduring happiness or misery, whether you can feel proud or ashamed of your boyfriend/girlfriend and yourself.

Whether your partner is really "cool" or sexy-looking becomes much less important than whether he/she is honest, sincere, trustworthy, hardworking, giving, unselfish, etc. We all know of countless Hollywood couples who rate on the top of the "Sexiest Man" or "Sexiest Woman in America" lists whose marriages broke up within just a few years.

As the PEA high of passion recedes, you will begin to see each other more realistically, with the strengths and weaknesses that all human beings have. The habits of relationship this person learned in his/her family will now be revealed more and more. Dr. Joel Bernstein, a New Jersey-based marriage counselor says that a mix of deep respect and a good sense of humor works best, "The teasing, and particularly a sense of playfulness, absorbs the aggression in relationships and fosters love."[10]

People who never achieve this third stage of intimacy, *connection*, are like leaves blowing in the wind, or like the shiny, windup toys mentioned in the story. They attract a lot of attention for a few hours, but break easily. They have no root and gravitate to this or that person for a while, but are never able to establish the love and intimacy which are based on real trust that comes with commitment.

In most cultures in the world, a couple shows their enduring committed love by getting married. While marriage ceremonies may differ because of religious or cultural differences, all known cultures in the world have the institution of marriage.

# The Fourth Stage of Intimacy: Caretaking

"It's the little things my wife does every day, because the little things are the hard things and they make you know someone is there. She's up every day, making breakfast for the kids and taking them to school. She's consistent and solid and full of discipline and dedication. I know it sounds corny, but I'm amazed by that."

Denzel Washington, *Mars and Venus*

"You'll never be happy if you can't figure out that loving people is all that there is. And that it's more important to love than to be loved. Because that is when you feel love, by loving somebody. I've learned that you get the rewards of love by giving love."

Gwyneth Paltrow, *Parade* magazine, January 17, 1999

The fourth stage of intimacy involves *caretaking.* Now the couple who spent much of their time in passionate embraces and long walks in the moonlight shifts their attention to the hoped-for birth of a child as a fruit of their love and a chance to pass onto future generations their ideals, traditions, and dreams.

Even though having children often means the shifting of time, resources, and energy from other goals, most parents find the sacrificial, caretaking role to be very rewarding as well as very challenging. The transformation of the couple into a family will change all of them forever.

After birth and while nursing, increased levels of oxytocin help to bond mother and child. The support and caring of the father relieve feelings of anxiety and concern for the future the mother may have.

There are sacrifices. Before the couple could spend their time and resources primarily to enjoy each other. Now they may spend much of their money on baby formula and diapers. They can barely remember the last time they could afford to go out to eat at a nice restaurant.

If they have not prepared their minds and hearts for these

sacrifices they may even become resentful towards the new child, blaming it for taking away their youthful freedom. We've all heard of tragic cases where a young parent takes out feelings of resentment on a child or abandons the child and other parent to seek "freedom."

Isn't such a turning away from one's own children and partner also turning away from oneself? Deep down, parents who abandon or abuse a child and a spouse must know they are turning away from one of the deepest fulfillments of being a man or a woman.

Yes, the lifelong commitment of getting married and becoming a parent may look like a mountain one hesitates to climb. Yet, as pointed out by Academy Award Winner Gwyneth Paltrow, when we pour ourselves out for another person, we learn what love really means. Mother Teresa, the woman who started homes for homeless people who were dying on the streets of Calcutta, once said that "Love hurts." And sometimes it does. But few who have experienced it would give it up for more passing pleasures.

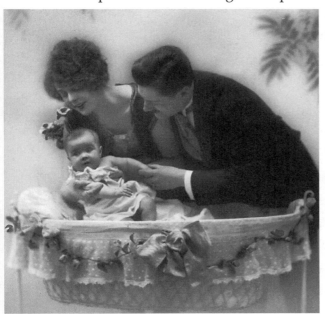

When we love in this unselfish way, our awareness of what life is about changes deeply.

It is fortunate that most parents have a natural desire and willingness to spend large amounts of time giving love and attention to their newborns and young children. The connection these children develop with their mothers and fathers will help them to develop empathy and sensitivity for the feelings of other human beings.[11] A special edition of *Newsweek* magazine with the title, "Your Child: From Birth to Three," reported that "cutting-edge science is confirming what wise parents have always known instinctively; young children need lots of time and attention from the significant adults in their lives."

The article goes on to state that "the long-term effects of inadequate nurturing can be devastating" and hamper brain development. Babies "who are hugged often and feel loved and cared for are much more likely to grow up confident and optimistic."[12] During World War II, doctors identified a mysterious, deadly disease they called "marasmus." It was discovered in a group of orphaned babies who were placed in an orphanage with brightly colored toys, new furniture, and good food. In spite of the good physical living conditions, the children were getting sicker and sicker. They stopped playing with their new toys and lost their appetites. Their tiny bodies weakened and some children died.

United Nations doctors were flown in to find out what was wrong. After a short time, the doctors prescribed a treatment which cured the problem within days: for ten minutes each hour, all children were to be picked up by a nurse, hugged, kissed, played with, and talked to. With this simple treatment, the infants became more lively, began to eat again and to play with their toys. Their "marasmus" was cured.[13]

The fourth stage of intimacy, caretaking, coincides with the crucial need of babies and young children for lots of time and attention from emotionally mature adults who are capable of giving them a loving, secure environment. The circle of love is made complete when we, who were once taken care of, now give our love, attention, and kindness to our own children. Their experience of love as children and in their friendships will prepare them for their future adult roles.

Think how strange it would be if parents kept a daily count of all the time and resources they spent on their children and gave those children a bill at the end of each year! Stranger still would be a baby who stopped his crying in the middle of the night and said to his parents, "You look really tired. I can wait until morning to be fed!" The parental, caretaking role is one of the greatest opportunities most of us will experience to learn the meaning of completely selfless, sacrificial love.

# Love: 3-Sided Triangle or 4-Sided House?

Robert Sternberg, a psychologist, has studied many couples to understand what love is. In his model, love is like a triangle. Its three sides are: passion, intimacy, and commitment. Passion, the strong desire for physical affection, usually occurs without much effort, particularly in the first stages of a relationship. Intimacy, the emotional element, requires both a willingness to open one's heart to another and the skills to communicate and to listen. If a couple lives without intimacy, they never get to know each other deeply and can never merge or bond. Commitment, the third side of the triangle, is based on the will and character of the couple and on their mature understanding of the importance of keeping their promises.[14]

A fourth element, compatibility, includes the shared interests, beliefs, values, and traditions of the couple. This provides common ground for the two so that their commitment is not just an act of will, but a shared agreement on the meaning and purpose of their marriage. That is why one needs to spend time getting to know someone before one rushes into marriage.

**Passion isn't enough**. It cannot last indefinitely.

Active participation in a shared religious faith is one factor that helps relationships. Among married couples, those who attend church more than once a month are twice as likely to stay married as couples who are less active.[15] Couples who initially are passionately in love often find out later that failing to understand each other's religious beliefs was a serious mistake.

Couples need to have shared interests and spend time together doing them. Otherwise they can become strangers, roommates sharing the same house. Intimacy, commitment, and compatibility are needed to create a marital house that won't fall apart when the first strong wind comes along.

That is why many engaged couples are being urged to take a premarital inventory and have counseling. They examine areas of agreement and disagreement on the many key issues that few couples "in love" think about until they're faced with the realities of financial pressures, different ideas about child-raising or even whether and when to have children.[16]

The four stages of intimacy are 1) attraction, 2) infatuation, 3) connection, 4) caretaking. Many people get stuck in stages one and two and never fulfill stages three and four. It's as if they are addicted to having certain feelings of excitement and passion. The minute those feelings begin to fade, they look for someone else. They are never able to achieve the deeper qualities of love that require sacrificial giving. Even as they hurt others because of their immaturity and self-centeredness, they hurt themselves by never growing up.

These four stages of intimacy are part of a larger life cycle-where we experience different qualities of love. First, as children we have an enormous hunger and capacity to receive love from our parents. This receptivity could be called *children's love.* As we grow older we form friendships on a more equal basis and begin to learn how to give, not just receive. We should also be learning how to relate to the opposite sex in brother/sister relationships. This second stage could be called *brother/sister love,* or more simply, *friendship.*

On the basis of having experienced children's love and real friendships we have the capacity to proceed through the four stages of intimacy and upon realizing them to enter into *marital love.* The 1998 movie *Ever After* in which Drew Barrymore played a dynamic "Cinderella" figure called Daniella displayed these four stages.

Daniella, whose mother died while giving birth to her, developed a strong bond with her father. On this foundation she was able to deal confidently with the opposite sex, including a boy she wrestled with as a child, and even the prince of France. The movie made it clear that sound romantic/marital love comes on the foundation of the two previous loves, children's love and brother/sister love. Developing these three loves prepares a couple for the sacrificial

Stages of Love and Intimacy

Attraction>Infatuation>Connection>Caretaking

Marital Love

Parents' Love

Children's Love

Friendship

love required in the stage of *parental love*.

Needless to say, if you want to achieve the mature form of love being described, thrusting yourself into possible premature parenthood by having uncommitted sex is the last thing you want to do. (See Appendix B for discussion of contraceptive failure rates.)

## The Human Search for *Meaning* in Sexuality

The well-known survivor of the Nazi concentration camps, Viktor Frankl, is best known for his book, *Man's Search for Meaning*. He also wrote extensively on the meaning of human sexuality.

In another book, *The Unheard Cry for Meaning: Psychotherapy and Humanism*, Frankl explains that all human sex is not necessarily human, especially if one treats it merely as a means of relieving sexual tensions, either by masturbating or through using a partner as a means to the same end. Such sex is neurotic, the act of someone who uses himself and others compulsively to achieve purely narcissistic (self-centered) ends. Frankl writes: "Only a neurotic individual is out first and foremost to get rid of his sperma, be it by masturbation or by using the partner as just another means to the same end."[17]

For Frankl, love means appreciating the unique value of another. In the sexual context, grasping the uniqueness of a loved one by definition would lead to a monogamous commitment, because no other could replace the loved one whose special identity is deeply felt. In contrast, promiscuity (having multiple sexual partners) means ignoring the other's uniqueness, because several partners are seen as interchangeable.

Imagine that you and your boyfriend/girlfriend are deeply in love. Because of the love you feel for each other, the two of you decide to go ahead and have sexual relations. A few days later you find out that your boyfriend/girlfriend is having sexual intimacy with someone else. Wouldn't you feel betrayed? Wouldn't you also think that your boyfriend/girlfriend is a real jerk and has selfishly treated you as an interchangeable sexual object, instead of making the same loving commitment you have made?

Being promiscuous, as Frankl points out, means being content with the partner as an object, *not as a person*. Such sex is not fulfilling, so people try to make up for the lack of quality with more quantity:

*Since only that sex which is embedded in love can be really rewarding and satisfactory, the quality of the sexual life of such an individual is poor. Small wonder, then, that he tries to compensate for this lack of quality with quantity. This, in turn, requires an ever increased and intensified stimulation, as is provided, for one, by pornography.*[18]

Frankl points out the hypocrisy in considering sexual promiscuity and pornography as "progressive" and "adult" since they are in reality symptoms of immaturity, signs of a lack of meaning in one's relationships. The more sex one gets, the less meaningful and satisfying it is:

*Like any other kind of inflation—e.g., that on the monetary market—sexual inflation is associated with a devaluation: sex is devaluated inasmuch as it is dehumanized. Thus, we observe a trend to living a sexual life that is not integrated into one's personal life, but rather is lived out for the sake of pleasure. Such a depersonalization of sex is a symptom of existential frustration: the frustration of man's search for meaning.*[19]

The 20th century sexual revolution promised better sex and more honesty and openness, but instead it has led to a legacy of broken hearts, more dishonesty, more alienation and an explosion in sexually transmitted diseases that has damaged millions of lives. As we enter the 21st Century, it's important that all of us clearly understand that free sex not only isn't free, but is based on fraudulent, unscientific claims about human sexuality. It is based on a profit-driven media industry that cares less about legitimate science and a lot about marketing a very profitable product, regardless of the human cost.

Our culture desperately needs to understand that more important than the sex drive is the *love drive*. It is only in the context of loving, committed relationships that most human beings find true sexual fulfillment. As the author and psychologist, Rollo May, once said: "The more powerful need is not sex per se but for relationships, intimacy, acceptance, and affirmation."

Science and technology have improved our lives in countless ways, but we must be careful not to view human beings in purely materialistic ways that envision them as little more than highly advanced animals. This is a demeaning point of view that truncates our understanding of the depth of the human potential for love.

1 Harville Hendrix, Ph.D., *Keeping the Love You Find: A Guide for Singles*, Simon and Schuster, New York, 1992.

2 This section based on article by Nicholas Wade, "Why Sex Works," *New York Times*, January 29, 1999.

3 Pat Love, Ph.D., 4125 Travis Country Circle, Austin, TX 78735.

4 Natalie Angier , "Study Finds Signs of Elusive Pheromones in Humans," *New York Times*, March 12, 1998.

5 PEA, phenylethylamine, an endogenous amphetamine, or "speed," is discussed in Robert L. Nadeau's book S/he Brain, Praeger Publishers, 1996.

6 Donald Orr, "Premature Sexual Activity as an Indicator of Psychosocial Risk," *Pediatrics,* 87:2, February 1991, 141-7.

7 Margery Williams, *The Velveteen Rabbit: or How Toys Become Real*, Doubleday, New York.

8 "The Science of Love," *Life* magazine, February 1999, 38-51.

9 Alan Feuer, "What's Love Got to Do With It?", *New York Times*, February 14, 1999.

10 Ibid.

11 Daniel Goleman, Emotional Intelligence, Bantam , New York, 1995, 102.

12 "Your Child: From Birth to Three," Newsweek, Spring/Summer 1997, New York.

13 Ashley Montague, "A Scientist Looks at Love," Phi Delta Kappa 11:9 (May 1970),
463-7, as discussed in Relationships by Les and Leslie Parrott.

14 Robert Sternberg, "A Triangular Theory of Love," *Psychological Review* 93, 1986, 119-35.

15 *National Survey of Family Growth,* National Institute of Child Development as reported in Michael McManus' *Marriage Savers,: Helping Your Friends and Family Stay Married*, Zondervan, Grand Rapids, MI, 1993, 122.

16 For more information about premarital counseling, contact: *Marriage Savers,* 9500 Michael's Court, Bethesda, MD 20817 / 301-469-5873.

17 Viktor E. Frankl, *The Unheard Cry for Meaning: Psychotherapy and Humanism*, Simon and Schuster, New York, 1978, 81.

18 Ibid., 82.

19 Ibid.

# Chapter Three

# Male

# &Female

*Living here far away*
*I am yours*
*Living there far away*
*You are mine*
*Love is not made*
*Of bodies only*
*Deep in the hearts*
*Is where we are one.*


Sanskrit Love Poem


*Men are like fine wine. They all start out like grapes,*
*and it's our job to stomp on them*
*and keep them in the dark*
*until they mature into something*
*we'd like to have dinner with.*


Anonymous woman

Through the ages the man/woman relationship has been a hotbed of contradictions–pleasure and pain, happiness and regret, desire and revulsion–or just plain skepticism, as in the quote from an anonymous woman above.

Religious symbolism tells us that men and women originally were one. A Greek myth recounted in Plato's *Dialogues* states that once there were beings who were both male and female who did something to anger the gods. Zeus' punishment was to divide each of them into two halves: one male, the other female. Ever since men and women have spent their whole lives searching for their other half. In the biblical tradition, as expressed in the Book of Genesis, it is said that the first woman was created from the rib of the man.

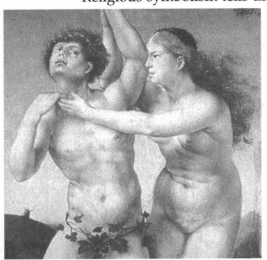

In both creation stories, the message is that man and woman were originally one, expressing the powerful attraction and deep longing that exists between the sexes.[1] Yet the book of Genesis also points to the likelihood of problems in male/female communication and shame in sexuality with Adam and Eve's eating of the fruit and being cast out of the "Garden of Eden," along with the covering of their nakedness.

In the 20th century, it became fashionable to believe that there were few inherent differences between the male and female gender other than the obvious physical ones. Research on the brain, however, is uncovering significant differences which begin in the womb. Computer-based imaging systems, such as positron emission tomography (PET) and magnetic resonance imaging (MRI), allow scientists to assess which areas of the brain are active. Studies based on these imaging systems have revealed that mental tasks in the female brain take place in both hemispheres of the brain, while the same tasks in the male brain take place in just one hemisphere.[2] Other studies show differences in the brain regions used by men and women to process language.

It is well-known that on average, girls speak more and earlier than boys. Girls tend to be more verbal and social and conscientious about their appearance. Boys speak much less than girls on average, although they sure can make a lot of noise! They are also more driven to prove their toughness and strength.[4]

Grownup males talk to give information or to report. They talk about things–business, sports, and food–rather than people. They convey facts, not details. They are goal-oriented. They focus on solving problems and are less likely to ask for help or directions. Males compete.

Females, on the other hand, talk to get information, to connect, or to develop a relationship. They talk about people rather than things. They convey feelings and details. They are quicker to ask for and accept help or directions. Women cooperate.[5]

Lillian Glass, a speech pathologist, author of *He Says, She Says: Closing the Communication Gap Between the Sexes,* has identified 105 gender differences in communication patterns involving five areas–body language, facial language, speech and voice patterns, content and behavior.[6]

In the bestseller *You Just Don't Understand: Women and Men in Conversation,* Deborah Tannen describes differences in male and female use of language. Men use conversation to assert their independence and status. Between men there is a lot of teasing banter and pseudo-putdowns that challenge each other's prowess. Women use conversation as "a way of establishing connections and negotiating relationships." Women are much more likely to talk about their feelings in order to establish empathy.

Men, Tannen says, tend to be more comfortable with public speaking, or *"report* talk," and women are usually more comfortable with private speaking, or *"rapport* talk." Men tend to use language that is abstract and categorical, with clear divisions. The language of women often conveys subtle nuances and hidden meanings. Men are likely to respond to problems with concrete solutions and suggestions; women respond with empathy and an emphasis on community and seeking consensus.[7]

The popular bestseller *Men Are From Mars, Women Are From Venus* by John Gray has similar themes. Gray imagines that men and women are races from two different planets. The Martians (men) value power, competency, efficiency, and achievement. They are always doing things to prove themselves and develop their power and skills. One's sense of self is defined through one's ability to achieve results.

Achieving goals is very important to a "Martian" because it is a way for him to prove his competence and thus feel good about himself. To feel good about himself, he must achieve these goals on his own. However, if he truly does need help, he will find someone he respects and talk about his problem. Another "Martian" feels honored by the opportunity to give advice. He puts on his "Mr. Fix-it" hat, listens for a while, and then offers some clear advice.

Gray says that this "Martian" custom is one of the reasons men instinctively offer solutions when women talk about problems. When a woman innocently shares feelings of upset or explores out loud the problems of her day, a man mistakenly assumes she is looking for some expert advice. He wants to be useful to her and feels that he can be valued and worthy of her love when he solves her problems.

Once he has offered a solution, however, and she continues to be upset, it becomes increasingly difficult for him to listen. His solution is being rejected. He feels useless. He does not know that on Venus talking about problems is not an invitation to offer a solution.

"Venusians" (women) have very different values. They value love, communication, beauty, and relationships. They spend a lot of time supporting, helping, and nurturing one another. Their sense of self is defined through their feelings and the quality of their relationships. They experience fulfillment through sharing and relating.

Everything on Venus reflects these values. Rather than building highways and tall buildings, the Venusians are more concerned with living together in harmony, community, and loving cooperation. Relationships are more important than work and technology. Communication is of primary importance. To share their personal feelings is much more important than achieving goals and success. Talking and relating to one another is a source of tremendous fulfillment.

Two "Martians" might go to lunch to discuss a project or business goal; they have a problem to solve. In addition, Martians view going to a restaurant as an efficient way to approach food: no shopping, no cooking, and no washing dishes. For Venusians, going to lunch is an opportunity to nurture a relationship, both giving and receiving support. Women's restaurant talk can be very open and intimate, almost like the dialogue that occurs between therapist and patient.

Venusians are very intuitive. They have developed this ability through centuries of anticipating the needs of others. They pride themselves in being considerate. A sign of great love is to offer help and assistance without being asked.

Because proving one's competence is not so important to a Venusian, offering help is not offensive, and needing help is not a sign of weakness. A man, however, may feel offended when a woman offers advice because he feels she does not trust his ability to do it himself. He feels that she is criticizing him when that wasn't her intention at all.

A reverse misunderstanding happens when a woman talks about her problems to a man. The man thinks she is looking for a "solution." He interrupts her to offer clear proposals about how to solve her problems, when all she is looking for is someone to listen empathetically. The act of sharing itself relieves her worries and anxieties.

Gray believes that many people mistakenly assume that if their boyfriends or girlfriends really love them, they will react and behave in the same ways that would be pleasing to themselves. For Gray, love means to accept that your partner may perceive and experience the world very differently than you do. Love involves learning to understand those differences and to act in ways that are pleasing and supportive to your partner.[8]

Some have expressed skepticism about Gray's sweeping statements about male and female natures. The popularity of his message is probably based on the implicit approval it gives for each to be different, however, and to accept that one's partner is different. Couples therapist David Schnarch calls this "differentiation," and says it is essential to real intimacy.[9] This kind of intimacy does not demand sameness of thought and action. It involves open-eyed awareness leading to stronger, more real intimacy with another person.

# A Darwinian View of Marriage

The institution of marriage in the U.S., while still chosen by the majority of American adults (56%), has suffered significant decline since 1970. Then, nearly 70% of adults were married. The decline came partly from an explosion in divorces. It was also a result of many 20 and 30-somethings postponing marriage to pursue education and careers. Fourteen million people between 25 and 34 years old (about 35% of Americans in that age group) have never married.[10]

It's always valuable to look at the big picture. How has marriage been looked at in history? What does the anthropological record tell us? A valuable resource for this purpose is Robert Wright's *The Moral Animal: The New Science of Evolutionary Psychology*. Wright tries to understand human behaviors in terms of their survival value.

Wright states that the institution of marriage exists in every known culture:

*In every human culture on the anthropological record, marriage—whether monogamous or polygamous, permanent or temporary—is the norm, and the family is the atom of social organization. Fathers everywhere feel love for their children, and that's a lot more than you can say for chimp fathers and bonobo fathers, who don't seem to have much of a clue as to which youngsters are theirs. This love leads fathers to help feed and defend their children, and teach them useful things. At some point, in other words, extensive male parental investment entered our evolutionary lineage.*[11]

Wright explains that unlike other animal species, human infants require many years of high male parental investment (MPI) in order to survive and prosper. That is why, he says, the promiscuous tendencies of many men to "spread their seed" among as many females as possible is tempered by concern that their children do well and survive, thus assuring the continuation of their lineage. For this to happen, men must decide to make a major life commitment to their children and to their children's mother.

Women on average tend to be much less promiscuous and more coy than men, for obvious reasons. Sex often leads to pregnancy, child-bearing and rearing. Women who were very selective about which male partners to allow sexual entry and who insisted upon male commitment to them and to their children (usually before the act of sex through a marriage ceremony) would tend to have healthier and more successful children than women who didn't insist upon male devotion.

What criterion would men use to decide which woman to devote much of their lives to? Wright states:

*If available females differ in their promiscuity, and if the more promiscuous ones tend to make less faithful wives, natural selection might incline men to discriminate accordingly. Promiscuous women would be welcome as short-term sex partners–indeed, preferable, in some ways, since they can be had with less effort. But they would make poor wife material, a dubious conduit for male parental investment.*[12]

What kind of emotional mechanisms, often unconscious, would lead men to make genetically advantageous investments and to avoid disadvantageous ones? For Wright, it is the much maligned but enduring "good girl-bad girl" or "Madonna-whore" dichotomy. This is the tendency of men to think in terms of "two kinds of women–the kind they respect and the kind they sleep with." Men, Wright says, tend to perform a mental calculus that goes something like this: "If she seems eager for sex right away, then by all means oblige her. But if the sex does come that easily, you might want to shift from investment mode into exploitation mode. Her eagerness could mean she'll always be an easy seduction–not a desirable quality in a wife."[13]

Wright's presentation of male/female relations is anything but politically correct and might seem curiously outdated and even morally reprehensible. Yet we will see that the chess game of male versus female he describes is very much with us as we near the 21st century. It is most evident in those communities where traditional sexual values have *the least impact on behavior.*

It's a sad reality that the offspring resulting from casual sexual relations get very little, if any, male parental investment. After all, men are less likely to invest time and resources if they're not sure if a child is theirs. The hard logic of natural selection prevails.

As an example of this tendency to withhold investment if the child is not theirs, Wright points to the Ache hunter-gatherers of

Paraguay. "Ache children raised by stepfathers after their biological fathers die are half as likely to live to age fifteen as children whose parents stay alive and live together."[14]

While sexual promiscuity has become much more accepted, especially in contemporary Western culture, the evolutionary logic described still operates. There is some level of female promiscuity above which male parental investment plainly makes no genetic sense. If a woman seems to have an unbreakable habit of sleeping with a different man each week, the fact that all women in that culture do the same thing doesn't make her any more logical a spouse. "In such a society," Wright says, "men should in theory give up entirely on concentrated parental investment and focus solely on trying to mate with as many women as possible. That is, they should act like chimpanzees."[15]

While contemporary culture in the developed Western nations has become much more accepting of unmarried sex, it is the continuing tendency of men to be very selective about whether and in whom to invest decades-long parental commitment. Wright is very aware that this apparently reactionary view of male/female relations will be discounted by many academics who see the Madonna-whore dichotomy as an aberration, evidence of the pathological depravity of Western culture.

In particular, the Victorians, with their extraordinary emphasis on virginity and their professed disdain for illicit sex, are held responsible for nourishing, even inventing, the pathology. If only men in Darwin's day had been more relaxed about sex, like the men in non-Western sexually liberated societies. But Wright points out, "the trouble is, those idyllic, non-Western societies seem to have existed only in the minds of a few misguided, if influential, academics who stress the malleability of the human species and assert the near absence of human nature."

As an example, Wright cites Margaret Mead, whose book, *Coming of Age in Samoa*, depicted "a culture nearly devoid of many Western evils: status hierarchies, intense competition, and all kinds of needless anxieties about sex." According to Wright, a 1983 book by anthropologist Derek Freman, *Margaret Mead and Samoa: The Making and Unmaking of an Anthropological Myth*, debunked Mead's research. Freman's book left Mead's reputation as a great anthropologist in serious disarray. He depicted her as a naïf, a 23 year-old idealist who went to Samoa steeped in fashionable cultural determinism, chose not to live among the natives, and then, dependent for her data on scheduled interviews, was duped by Samoan girls who made a game of misleading her.

In place of Mead's vision of a Samoan society with little male jealousy or possessiveness, or any male concern whatsoever about female promiscuity, Freeman explains that a Samoan woman found on her wedding day not to be a virgin was publicly denounced with a term meaning, roughly, "whore." A song performed at defloration ceremonies went like this: "All others have failed to achieve entry, all others have failed to achieve entry. He is first by being foremost, being first he is foremost; O to be foremost!"[16] Wright explains that some of the more harsh Samoan penalties for non-virgins had if anything been suppressed by Western influence.

For Wright, one of the strongest candidates for "human nature" is the already mentioned "good girl-bad girl" dichotomy, a reputation for extreme promiscuity actively avoided by men in a long-term mate. It is to be found in exotic cultures from Samoa to Mangaia to the land of the Ache in South America, in the Far East, in Islamic states, in Europe, even in pre-Columbian America.[17]

It isn't just the anthropological record that supports the "good girl-bad girl" paradigm. Psychological research, says Wright, has found evidence that men do dichotomize between short-term and long-term mates. Cues suggesting promiscuity (a low-cut dress, perhaps, or aggressive body language) make a woman more attractive as a short-term mate and less attractive as a long-term mate. Cues suggesting a lack of sexual experience work the other way around.[18]

The point here is not to blame so-called "bad women," but rather to help young women to see where their true self-interest lies. If they are interested in long-term, serious, respectful and committed relationships with men, sexual liberation is not the way to go.

## Monogamous Marriage Reduces Violence

Wright points out that the vast majority of men, even in polygamous cultures, cannot afford more than one wife. Monogamy is a democratic practice in the sense that most men will be able to find a wife; whereas in highly despotic societies, a few men, especially the ruler, would be able to have an unlimited number of wives, causing a deficit among less powerful men.[19]

Monogamy is not just democratic. It has other social benefits. Wright explains that leaving lots of men without wives and children is not just inegalitarian, it's dangerous. The ultimate source of the danger is sexual selection among males. Men have long competed for access to the scarcer sexual resource, women. And the costs of losing the contest are so high (genetic oblivion) that natural selection has inclined them to compete with special ferocity.

Fortunately, Wright points out, male violence can be dampened by circumstance, one of which is a mate: "We would expect womanless men to compete with special ferocity, and they do. An unmarried man between 24 and 35 years of age is about three times as likely to murder another male as is a married man the same age. Some of this difference no doubt reflects the kinds of men that do and don't get married to begin with, but Martin Daly and Margo Wilson have argued cogently that a good part of the difference may lie in 'the pacifying effect of marriage.' "[20, 21]

Murder isn't the only thing an "unpacified" man is more likely to do. He is also more likely to incur various risks–committing robbery, for example–to gain the resources that may attract women. He is more likely to rape. This is perhaps the best argument for monogamous marriage, with its egalitarian effects on men: inequality among males is more socially destructive–in ways that harm women and men. A polygynous (where males have many female partners) nation, in which large numbers of low-income men remain mateless, is not the kind of country many of us would want to live in.

Unfortunately, Wright points out, this is the sort of country we already live in. "Whereas in 1960 the fraction of the population age forty or older that had never married was about the same for men and women, by the 1990s the fraction was markedly larger for men than for women. It is not crazy to think that there are homeless alcoholics and rapists who, had they come of age in a pre-1960s social climate, amid more equally distributed female resources, would early on have found a wife and adopted a lower-risk, less destructive lifestyle."[22]

It is tragically ironic that while many feminists denounced marriage as a patriarchal, anti-democratic institution that oppressed women, the cultural shift away from marriage has led to much higher rates of violence in communities where married couples are an endangered species. Tragically, it is unmarried women who suffer the highest rates of domestic violence.[23]

Much has been said about the declining well-being of children in

many countries and in what some call the "underclass" in the U.S. A *Save the Children* rally in Washington, D.C. in 1996 focused attention on the plight of many of these children. But curiously lacking was any attempt by rally organizers to discuss the causes of declining well-being of children. In most cases, it was the absence of their fathers.

A Darwinian view of parental motives may provide a bitter clarity. Substitute parents will generally tend to care less profoundly for children than natural parents. Children reared by people other than their natural parents will be more often exploited and otherwise at risk. Parental investment is a precious resource, and selection must favor those parental psyches that do not squander it on nonrelatives.[24]

Martin Daly and Margo Wilson point out that an American

child living with one or more substitute parents was about one hundred times more likely to be fatally abused than a child living with natural parents. In a Canadian city in the 1980s, a child two years of age or younger was seventy times more likely to be killed by a parent if living with a stepparent and one natural parent than if living with two natural parents. Children under ten were, depending on their age and the particular study in question, between three and forty times more likely to suffer parental abuse if living with a stepparent and a natural parent than if living with two natural parents.[25]

Other less dramatic, undocumented forms of parental indifference follow this rough pattern, says Wright. Fathers give their children all kinds of tutelage and guidance (more, often, than either father or child realizes) and guard them against all kinds of threats. A mother alone simply can't pick up the slack. A stepfather almost surely won't pick up much of it.

Reality is that the best caretakers and advocates for children are most often their *own natural parents*. Furthermore, the idea that government intervention can fill in the void created by fatherless families or protect women and children from increased rates of male violence related to family breakdown is ultimately a cruel hoax.

Some would argue that you can have it both ways. Young people can afford to experiment with sex while they are young and active and then "settle down" when they get a little older. Aside from the fact they may pick up one or two of two dozen common sexually transmitted diseases (see Appendix A), it's questionable if sexual experience with different partners will really help their future relationships. Wright points out that Victorian advocacy of premarital chastity has a practical wisdom independent of purely religious or moral rationales: If it is harder to drag men to the altar today than it used to be, one reason is that they don't have to stop there on the way to the bedroom. If a Madonna-whore switch is indeed built into men's brains, men are much less likely to "settle down" with women who grant premarital sexual favors.[26]

But sexual attitudes of men and women do not operate in a vacuum. They are affected by perceptions of what the opposite sex "wants," perceptions that may be based on things that have little to do with real human needs and something as crass and money-driven as billboard campaigns by Calvin Klein, advertizing in magazines, and plotlines in TV or movies. Slight changes in the culture in the "right" direction can lead to more positive, less exploitative changes in attitudes, and behavior: "The more Madonnaish the women, the more daddish and less caddish the men, and thus the more Madonnaish the women, and so on."[27]

In an age when "pursuing one's sexuality" and "sexual rights" are seen as indisputable as constitutional rights, it's easy to look back with pity or contempt on the "sexually repressed" Victorians in a less liberated age, but thirty years of obedience to our sexual impulses as if they were the voice of the Noble Savage has led to: "lots of fatherless children; lots of embittered women; lots of complaint about date rape and sexual harassment; and the frequent sight of lonely men renting X-rated videotapes while lonely women abound."[28] It's debatable which age is more pitiable. Maybe the Victorians had it right after all.

# Male/Female Differences Today

The Sexual Revolution convinced many women that saving sex for marriage was an old-fashioned relic of male-dominated society. Even so there are strong persisting differences in attitudes between men and women which would indicate an institution that mediates between them such as marriage is still needed. Several years ago a study was done at the University of Hawaii. Attractive male and female interviewers asked students of the opposite sex one of three questions: "Would you go on a date with me?"; "Would you go to my apartment?"; and "Would you have sex with me?"

Equal numbers, 50% of the male and female students, said yes to a date. In response to being asked if they would agree to go to the questioner's apartment, 94% of the females said no, while 7 out of 10 men said yes. In response to the last question about having sex, 100% of the women said no, while 3 out of 4 men said yes.[29]

Of course, women have to worry about issues like pregnancy and personal safety more than men do. For these and other reasons we continue to  see, 30 years after the Sexual Revolution, an enormous ongoing difference in male and female attitudes about sex, particularly with people they don't know well.

Another gender difference: death rates for men are much higher than for women. The death rate from accidents is 3 times higher for men, and 5 times higher for homicide and suicide among men ages of 16 to 24. The higher death rates persist for middle-aged and older men as well, although the causes of death are usually from disease. Part of the reason for higher death rates is that men are much more risk-taking and more reckless than women.

When we examine the male population alone, we find that there are vast differences between single men and married men. Single men die at twice the rate of married men from all causes, are ten times more likely to be hospitalized for chronic diseases, and 22 times more likely to be committed to an institution for mental disease.[30]

Single men are more violent, on average. Single men are only

13% of the population over age 14, but they commit nearly 90% of the violent crimes.[31] It is ironic that feminists in the '60s and '70s railed at marriage as a den of domestic violence and said that male domination, particularly in marriage, was the root of violence, when the truth is that marriage usually channels male aggression in more positive directions.

## "Living Together" Versus Commitment

According to FBI reports, women with a live-in lover are sixty times more likely to be physically abused than women who live with their husbands.[32] The FBI also reports that men and women who never married are four times more likely to be victims of violence.[33] These figures are in sharp contrast to the way the mass media presents the issue of domestic violence. Several years ago, **many national TV networks gravely warned viewers that research showed that during Superbowl Sunday rates of domestic violence against wives greatly increased. The research didn't exist, but was broadcast because it fit in with contemporary cultural bias against marriage.**

Some say that at the beginning of the 21st century we must not be so small-minded as to think that getting married is the only, or even the best, arrangement for a man and a woman to live together. Many couples just live together. The trend of living together without marriage, sometimes called cohabitation , is soaring. By 1998, the number of unmarried U.S. couples topped 4,236,000, up from 439,000 in 1960, according to the Census Bureau. More than half of first marriages are now preceded by cohabitation, says David Popenoe, a Rutgers University sociologist.[34] Many 20-somethings think that one good way to find out if someone would make a good marriage partner is to live with that person–to see if you're compatible sexually and otherwise.

This sounds reasonable, but one problem in unmarried living arrangements is that neither partner can really be sure about the other partner's commitment. One may be expecting or hoping for marriage, hoping to convince the other to make a commitment, but the other may see their living arrangement as a convenient way to get the benefits of marriage (companionship, sex, shared housekeeping) without the hassles.

Others say that marriage is good for men and bad for women. Living together provides a quicker escape hatch in case the woman realizes that she is losing more than she is gaining. But, as the following article shows, living together has higher costs and less benefits than its advocates realize:

# COHABITORS REPORT LESS BLISS THAN MARRIED COUPLES

**Fox News,** New York, August 24, 1998

*Couples who live together long-term without "tying the knot" are more depressed and less satisfied with their lives than their married peers, according to a report based on data from the 1987-1988 National Survey of Families and Households. In particular, women with children are most likely to feel depression if they are cohabiting rather than married, according to the study presented Saturday at the American Sociological Association meeting in San Francisco. This dissatisfaction and depression may stem from the instability of the union, according to study author Dr. Susan Brown, an assistant professor of sociology at Bowling Green State University in Ohio. "We know that cohabiting unions are much less stable than marital unions, and I think that has a significant impact on their depression and life satisfaction levels," she said in an interview with Reuters Health.*

Of course, many couples who live together end up getting married. But research shows that couples who live together before getting married have lower quality marriages on average and a higher risk of divorce.[35] Couples who live together before marriage are nearly 50% more likely to divorce than those who don't, say David Popenoe and Barbara Dafoe Whitehead. They are co-directors of the National Marriage Project, a think tank at Rutgers University in New Jersey, and co-authors of a study titled, "Should We Live Together? What Young Adults Need to Know About Cohabitation Before Marriage."

Among the recent studies on cohabitation and marriage was one released in 1997 by the National Center for Health Statistics. It showed that 27% of women who lived with someone before getting married ended up divorced within five years. In contrast, ten percent of women who never lived with a boyfriend saw their marriages dissolve in the same period.[36]

Their review of almost 50 studies of cohabiting couples showed that living together is apparently not the best way to prepare for marriage. People who live together outside of marriage are less likely to see marriage as a special, unique commitment. Popenoe and Whitehead say that it's wrong to assume you learn how to have good relationships by cohabiting for three reasons:

- The more a person cohabits, the more likely the person is to embrace cohabiting as a lifestyle.

- The longer people live together without marriage, the more likely it is that they'll never marry. A series of cohabitations could become their lifestyle.

- Cohabiting parents break up at a much higher rate than married parents, and the economic and emotional effects of the breakup can be devastating on children. They point out that, "Fully three quarters of children born to cohabiting parents will see their parents split up before they reach age 16, whereas only about a third of the children born to married parents face a similar fate."

Another risk for the children of cohabitors is the higher rate of child abuse. Popenoe and Whitehead point to a study in Britain which found that children living with cohabiting couples are 20 times more likely to be the subject of child abuse. In cases in which the child is living with a mother and a man who is not the father, the risk increases 33 times.

The negative effects of cohabiting are lessened only when there is a marriage date on the horizon, and not on the distant horizon.[37]

On average, research shows that married people have:

- better physical and emotional health
- longer life expectancy
- higher incomes

This is in comparison to people who have never married or who have divorced or separated or unmarried couples who live together.[38]

Dr. Linda Waite at the University of Chicago has found that "marriage changes people's behavior in ways that make them better off." Married partners monitor each other's health, for example.

They also drink less alcohol and have lower usage of marijuana and cocaine.

From detailed reports on 50,000 men and women followed from their senior year in high school to the age of 32 by University of Michigan researchers, Dr. Waite discerned a steep increase in "bad behaviors" among those who stayed single, but a "precipitous drop" in bad behaviors like the use of alcohol or illegal drugs among those who married. She also found that married men and women experience higher levels of happiness compared to those who remained single or who separated or divorced.[39]

And, contrary to what *Playboy* and *Penthouse* would have us believe, married men and women are more sexually fulfilled on average than those who aren't married. Unmarried couples living together had just as much sex, but were less *emotionally satisfied*. Those with more than one sexual partner in the past year were the *least* emotionally satisfied.[40] The higher rates of sexual satisfaction are probably due to the greater amount of trust that exists in most marriages. They don't have to worry as much that their partner

*MAYBE THAT'S WHY THE MORE I GOT, THE LESS FULFILLED I WAS.*

will leave for someone else the next day, or week or month. The couple has time to learn how to please each other and more motivation to do so than someone involved in a short-term relationship or a one-night stand. They feel less pressure to give a perfect "performance" since they aren't being evaluated and compared with other possible partners. The commitment has already been made. They will probably have years to reach their prime.

A famous survey of 100,000 women sponsored by *Redbook* magazine found that strictly monogamous women experienced orgasm twice as often as women who were promiscuous. Women who were sexually active as teens expressed much more dissatisfaction with their sex lives as adults.[41] The idea that it's beneficial or even necessary to have sexual experiences before marriage in order to achieve sexual satisfaction within marriage is simply not true.

The most scientific sex survey ever, conducted at the University of Chicago and dominating the covers of *Newsweek, Time,* and other national media, found that women who were strictly monogamous and who held traditional values regarding sex were more likely to report higher sexual fulfillment than those who had more permissive values or sexual partners previous to marriage.[42] Having sex with more than one partner means that you've bonded with more than one partner. Unless you've totally detached your emotion from the experience of physical intimacy, your heart and mind are somewhat divided.

A good example of this is Mike, a man who is totally in love with his wife and has no desire whatsoever for other women. His problem is that every time he is making love to his wife he sees the faces of previous female sex partners he had before he got married. Haunted by his past, he feels he has never been truly alone in bed with the woman he loves.

Other research findings:

• A University of South Carolina study revealed that people who engaged in premarital sex were more likely to be involved in extramarital affairs after marriage.[43]

• Men and women who lived together with someone before marriage are also more likely to get involved in adultery after marriage than men and women who didn't do this.[44]

• Research also shows women who save sex for marriage have higher rates of marital success and are less likely to get divorced.[45]

The ones who were willing to wait probably placed a higher value on marriage and made a stronger commitment to it. As with many things in life, it's a question of one's priorities.

Despite the added financial costs married couples face in terms of housing and raising a family, it has been found that married couples have four times as much wealth as single or divorced people.[46] The average income of married-parent households whose heads have only a high school diploma is ten percent higher than the median income of college-educated single-parent households.[47] If we truly hope to address poverty in America, marriage would seem to be just as important as education in preparing people for a decent living.

These economic advantages come in large part because of the bonds of mutual support between the married couple and their extended families. The relatives of the married couple are often more willing to help the couple financially when they are married than when they aren't.

Married couples tend to be more productive at work, probably because they know there's someone at home who believes in and encourages them. They also know there are others depending on them. For that reason, married couples are much less likely to engage in risky or self-destructive behavior such as violence or drug abuse. Most married men and women have turned their backs on immature and destructive behavior. The benefits to their own children and to the communities in which they live are obvious.

These research results stand in stark contrast to what advo-

cates of sexual freedom promised. Instead of more sexual fulfillment, "swinging singles" get less. Instead of greater emotional satisfaction, they are less emotionally fulfilled. Instead of more freedom, many find themselves trapped in poverty.

In the minds of many, marriage is desired but also feared. It represents a closing off of options, of choices.

"What if I meet someone better?" they think. "If we just live together, I can always leave if things turn negative," they tell themselves.

Besides the statistical odds against cohabiting couples forming a viable and permanent union, the commitment of marriage is a life-transforming one. One of the best explanations why marriage is preferable to living together with an escape hatch comes from author and marriage therapist Harville Hendrix who explains:

H
H

"The ingredients necessary for full growth and healing—attention, concentration, security, time, deepest intimacy, and full mirroring of ourselves—are possible only in marriage. We cannot heal ourselves, and we cannot heal in open-ended, precarious relationships."

Are men transformed by marriage? Are male tendencies towards aggressiveness, recklessness and promiscuity changed by a long-term commitment to a woman? The man is asked in marriage to sacrifice the joys of "new conquests," and to settle down for life and to "be responsible." Admittedly, this is a scary thought for a lot of guys.

But a man *gains* by entering the emotional universe of intimacy with a woman and with children that would otherwise be inaccessible.[48] Another way of saying it is that *he becomes necessary*. A single man can do whatever he wants, even things which might get him killed, and it may not concern him very much. But a married man must evaluate *every action* in terms of how it may affect his family.

There are other reasons most adults choose to get married even when society minimizes the importance of marriage. The reason is that the human desire for intimacy, to be fully known and to fully know another, cannot be fulfilled in a half-hearted, half-way relationship. It's like flying in an airplane. *You have to be all the way in* or you'll never get off the ground!

If you have any experience as a lifeguard, you know that people usually drown because they panic and expend a lot of energy trying to raise their bodies out of the water. They become so exhausted that they drown. If they relaxed and accepted being in the water, their bodies would naturally come to the right level for floating. In a similar way, many people are afraid of making a lifelong marital commitment. Fearing the worst about what might go wrong, they always keep an escape hatch open in their minds, but this damages their ability to grow into deeper love.

As the poet Elizabeth Barrett Browning put it, "I love you not for what you are but for what I am with you." A permanent love partner is an opportunity for growth. The more one works to love a partner who is not always very loveable, the more one learns what love really is. As author and counselor Edward Ford points out in his excellent book, *Permanent Love:*

*"Marriage gives you nothing more than a fighting chance to make a lover of yourself," and not just in bed, but in your life...your love for others will come more from your efforts to love them than from the love they give you, as important as that is. Childhood is the last, the only, occasion where we grow from passively receiving human love; thereafter the obligation shifts to our shoulders and stays there."[49]*

We live in a throw-away society. After something (or someone) outlives its usefulness, it gets thrown away. Once we encounter difficulties in a relationship, increasing numbers of people simply choose to end it. Harville Hendrix points out that ending relationships, or getting a divorce, doesn't necessarily lead to new and better relationships or marriages: "We have given credence to the idea that when trouble comes you should just change partners, when the truth is that the way you are living with that person must be changed. *Rather than getting rid of the partner and keeping the problem, you should get rid of the problem so that you can keep the partner."[50]*

In fact, people who divorce and remarry are more likely to divorce again. Romantic love, Hendrix points out, "is supposed to end. It is nature's glue, which brings two incompatible people together for mutual growth. When romantic love dies, as it must, it clears the way for real love. The creation of real love is nature's way of repairing and completing itself—through you."[51]

Some will argue that staying married to an abusive husband or to a spouse who has a persistent drug abuse problem who refuses or is unable to change is wrong and dangerous, and they're right. But according to one study, physical abuse plays a role in only 5% of divorce cases; drug or alcohol abuse leads to 16% of divorces. Poor communication and conflict resolution skills lead to 57% of divorces.[52] The couples didn't know how to manage disagreements or at least how to balance them out with positive shared activities. Since communication skills can be learned that means that potentially more than half of all divorces in the U.S. could be prevented.

Programs for engaged and for newly married couples called PREPARE and ENRICH used detailed attitude surveys that can predict with 80% accuracy which couples will succeed in marriage. The main predictors include:

1) realistic expectations,
2) personality issues such as optimism and stability,
3) abilities to communicate and to resolve the inevitable disagreements that arise in every marriage,
4) religious orientation.

Couples who have weaknesses in these key areas are encouraged to delay marriage so that they can work on their weak points.[53] Some couples, who have become aware of their fundamental disagreements on important issues, decide not to get married at all.

Marriage therapists like Michele Weiner-Davis have had tremendous success in saving troubled marriages. Her approach is that "relationships are such that if one person makes significant changes, the relationship must change. Too many marriages go down the drain because each spouse is waiting for the other to change first."[54]

One woman put it this way: "For the first ten years of our marriage, I saw his faults and tried to change them, but failed miserably. Then I changed my attitude. My husband isn't perfect, he's balding and has got a paunch, but he'd work nine days a week to support our family and I love him. We're much happier now."

The point is, while every relationship goes through ups-and-downs, there are proven ways to strengthen marriages. Ask any couple that's been married for more than twenty years whose relationship you admire if they ever went through rough times. Their answer will surely be yes. Yet if they had thrown in the towel during the rough times, they might be like so many other lonely divorcees and wouldn't have achieved their current happiness.

## Bad Reasons to Get Married

*If I am attached to another person because I cannot stand on my own two feet, he or she may be a life saver, but the relationship is not one of love.*

Erich Fromm

While it is clear that marriage provides many benefits for the great majority of those who choose it, it would be foolish indeed to think that getting married for its own sake is a good idea! There are bad reasons to get married that anyone contemplating it should be aware of and avoid.

Some people get married for very unrealistic reasons or as an escape from a current situation that is unpleasant. This might be an unhappy relationship with one's parents or just feeling depressed. But no matter how great marriage is, it can't replace the hard work of personal growth. Les and Leslie Parrott, who counsel married couples, put it this way: "Marriage does not erase personal pain or eliminate loneliness. Why? Because people get married primarily to further their own well-being, not to take care of their partners' needs. The bad traits and feelings you carried around before you were married remain with you as you leave the wedding chapel. A marriage certificate is not a magical glass slipper."

Another poor reason to get married is the false belief that "my spouse will make me whole." Marriage does challenge us to new heights and does call us to be the best person possible, but neither marriage nor our partner will magically make us whole. Persons with such a belief become dependent on their partner for continual support and assurance.

Another common myth is that if we just find "Mr. Right" or "Ms. Right" everything will be fine. But nothing replaces the hard work of building a marriage based on accepting the real human being you've actually married.[55] Many people use romantic love the way a drunk uses a street lamp–not for light, but for support.[56]

Many people want to leave a marriage, saying, "I don't love her (or him) anymore," as if love were born, not made. A person who cannot love one partner in all likelihood will have trouble loving another. Instead of "I cannot love her (or him)," it should be, "I cannot love. I do not know how to love." Then the person should learn and practice the art of loving. It may turn out that the same old partner, when loved, is Mr. or Ms. Right after all.

[1] Joseph Campbell, *The Power of Myth,* Doubleday, New York, 1988, 6.

[2] S.P. Springer and G. Deutsch, Left Brain, Right Brain, W. H. Friedman Co., San Francisco, 1985.

[3] Ruben Gur, quoted in Gina Kilota, "Men's World, Women's World? Brain Studies Point to Differences," New York Times, February 28, 1995, C1.

[4] Patricia and Peter Adler, "Peer Power: Culture and Identity," as reported in article by Kay S. Hymowitz, "Kids Today Are Growing Up Way Too Fast," *Wall Street Journal,* October 28, 1998.

[5] Marilyn A. Sachs, "Male/Female Communication Styles," *Ohio State University Extension Factsheet,* Family and Consumer Sciences, 1787 Neil Ave., Columbus, OH 43210.

[6] Lillian Glass, Ph.D., *He Says, She Says: Closing the Communication Gap Between the Sexes,* Putnam Publishing Group, New York, 1993.

[7] Deborah Tannen, You Just Don't Understand: Women and Men in Conversation, New York, Ballantine Books, 1990, 77.

[8] John Gray, Ph.D., Men are from Mars, Women are from Venus, HarperCollins Publishers, New York, 1992.

[9] David Schnarch, Ph.D., *Passionate Marriage: Keeping Love & Intimacy Alive in Committed Relationships,* Henry Holt & Co., New York, 1997.

[10]*Associated Press,* "Marrieds remain majority, but percentage continues to decline," January 7, 1999

[11] Robert Wright, *The Moral Animal: Evolutionary Psychology and Everyday Life,* Random House, New York, 1994, 57-8.

[12] Ibid., 72.

[13] Ibid.

[14] Ibid., 69.

[15] Ibid., 74.

[16] Derek Freeman, *Margaret Mead and Samoa: the Making and Unmaking of an Anthropological Myth*, Cambridge, MA: Harvard University Press, 1983.

[17] Ibid., 74-8.

[18] David Buss and D.P. Schmitt, "Sexual Strategies Theory: an Evolutionary Perspective on Human Mating," *Psychological Review*, 100: 204-32, 1993.

[19] Laura Betzig, *Despotism and Differential Reproduction: A Darwinian View of History*, Aldine de Gruyter, New York, 1986.

[20] Martin Daly and Margo Wilson, *Homicide*, Aldine de Bruyter, Hawthorne, N.Y., 1988.

[21] Martin Daly and Margo Wilson, "Killing the Competition: Female/Female and Male/Male Homicide," *Human Nature*, 1:81-107, 1990.

[22] Ibid.

[23] National Crime Victimization Survey, conducted by the U.S. Justice Dept., as discussed in David Blankenhorn's *Fatherless America*, 35-6.

[24] Daly and Wilson, *Homicide*, op cit., 83.

[25] Ibid., 89-91.

[26] Robert Wright, op cit., 122-3.

[27] Ibid., 141.

[28] Ibid., 145.

[29] Robert White, "Our Cheating Hearts," *Time*, August 15, 1994.

[30] U.S. National Center for Health Statistics, *Vital Statistics of the United States*, annual; and *Monthly Vital Statistics Report.*

[31] George Gilder, *Men and Marriage*, Pelican, Gretna, LA, 1992, 64-5.

[32] 1992 U.S. Justice Dept. Study "Female Victims of Violent Crime."

[33] U.S. Dept. of Justice report on "Sex Differences in Violent Victimization, 1994," September, 1997.

[34] Karen S. Peterson, "Cohabitation has big downside, study finds ," *USA Today*, February 1, 1999.

[35] A. DeMaris and K.V. Rao, "Premarital Cohabitation and Subsequent Marital Stability in the U.S.: a reassessment," *Journal of Marriage and the Family 54*, February, 1992, 178-190.

[36] Michelle Boorstein, "Living Together–Divorce Link Found,"

Associated Press, February 2, 1999.

[37] Charles M. Madigan, "Marriage 101: Skip the Trial Run," *Tribune,* February 1, 1999.

[38] Beth Hahn, "Marital Status and women's health: the effect of economic acquisitions," *Journal of Marriage and the Family 55,* May 1993, 495-504.

[39] Hara E. Marano, "Debunking the Marriage Myth: It Works for Women, Too," *New York Times,* August 4, 1998.

[40] Robert T. Michael, *Sex in America, a definitive survey,* Little, Brown, and Company, Boston, 1994.

[41] *Redbook Survey on Female Sexuality,* Vol. 145, September 1975, 54.

[42] Robert T. Michael, op cit.

[43] L.H. Bukstel, et al., "Projected Extramarital Sexual Involvement in Unmarried College Students," *Journal of Marriage and the Family 40,* 1978, 337-40.

[44] M.D. Newcomb and P.M. Bentler, "Assessment of Personality and Demographic Aspects of Cohabitation and Marital Success," *Journal of Personality Assessment 44,* 1980, 21.

[45] J.R. Kahn, K.A. London, "Premarital Sex and the Risk of Divorce," *Journal of Marriage and the Family 53,* November 1991, 845-55.

[46] Statistical Abstract of the United States, U.S. Bureau of Census, 1993, 113th edition, Washington, D.C., 385.

[47] Analysis of income data provided by The Northeastern University Center for Labor Market Studies as reported in Barbara Dafoe Whitehead's *The Divorce Culture,* Random House, New York, 1996, 8.

[48] George Gilder, *Naked Nomads: Unmarried Men in America,* Quadrangle/ NY Times Book Company, New York, 1974, 153.

[49] Edward E. Ford, *Permanent Love: practical steps to a lasting relationship,* Brandt Publishing, Scottsdale, AZ, 1979, 78.

[50] Harville Hendrix, *Keeping the Love You Find: a Guide for Singles,* Simon and Schuster, New York, 1992, 22.

[51] Ibid., 230.

[52] Gallup poll as reported in *Marriage Savers,* ibid., 122.

[53] Ibid., 114.

[54] Michele Weiner-Davis, *Divorce Busting,* Summit Books, New York, 1992.

[55] Les and Leslie Parrott, *Saving Your Marriage Before It Starts,* Zondervan Publishing House, Grand Rapids, 1995, 24-27.

[56] Edward E. Ford, *op cit.,* 62.

# Comprehending

## the

# Chapter four

# Culture

None of us live in a vacuum. For good or ill, we are all influenced by messages coming into our hearts and minds from others. Every time we see a billboard, a magazine cover, a TV show, a movie, listen to the radio or a music CD, log onto the Internet, or just talk to a friend, we are being influenced.

As we approach the beginning of the 21st century, it's important to understand why and how the easing of traditional values regarding sex came about. What influences and which minds have shaped the cultural shift away from the ideal of reserving sex for marriage–the Sexual Revolution? [1]

As we look at the flow of thought about sexuality down through the centuries, it is clear that two competing philosophies have shaped our attitudes. From the beginning these philosophies have been vying for dominance, not only in culture, but in individuals' lives. Surprisingly though, in spite of their opposition, each has contributed important elements to our understanding of sexual issues today.

The first stream of thought on sexuality has been shaped largely by the major religions of the world. Their message is overwhelmingly that sex is a very special gift from the Creator, to be used within certain guidelines. If we do not use it within those limits, it can cause much pain and heartache. All the major religions of the world agree that sex should be reserved for marriage.

For example, Judeo-Christian writings say the following: "For this cause a man shall leave his father and his mother, and shall cleave to his wife; and they shall become one flesh."[2] In the Song of Solomon of the Hebrew Bible or Old Testament we have many joyful, exuberant passages about sex within marriage.[3] The Puritans who fled Europe to practice their Christian faith in America also praised the delights of married love.[4]

Buddhism has five major precepts, one of which is sexual purity. The Dalai Lama is today's most prominent Buddhist, and he writes very clearly of marriage being the place for sex.[5] It is of interest that Hinduism also holds five rules to be of highest value. One rule, to not engage in adultery, includes premarital sexual activity.[6]

Many people are aware of the Muslim laws against sex outside of marriage. Few Westerners know that Muhammad encouraged enjoyment of sex by both husband and wife, and once called intercourse without concern for the woman's pleasure a form of cruelty to women. Most do not know that Islam is one of the few religions to include sex as one of the rewards in the afterlife.[7]

As far as most major faiths and religions are concerned, there is no disagreement that sex should be enjoyed in the context of a faithful, monogamous marriage.

The influence of religion on sexual practice has been

profound, and most of this influence has been protective to individuals in society. Those who practiced sexual activity according to the rules of their faith had intercourse only with their wife or husband for life. This provided nearly perfect protection against sexually transmitted disease and nonmarital pregnancy. There were other benefits from this practice, primarily for the woman. For example, she was usually not without a mate to help provide for and raise her children.

Even though not all people around the world have been or are now adherents to religious belief, there have been enormous benefits from the influence of the various major faiths. They have been the source from which our concepts of character concerning the value of the individual, respect, responsibility, self-control, and delayed gratification have come. These and others are the universal core ethical values that allow diverse peoples to live together in harmony and which allow for physically and emotionally healthier sex.

The second stream of thought challenged the widespread agreement among world religions about reserving sex for marriage and criticized them for denying people free access to sexual information. The human eugenics movement, which became influential in the 19th and early 20th century, was rooted in a pessimistic view of history first expressed in 1798 by Thomas Malthus. Malthus theorized that a population will always grow at a faster rate than its means of production, leading inevitably to poverty, famines and wars.

Eugenicists claimed that to avoid such calamities the human race must begin the selective breeding of human beings. Social Darwinists, who applied Darwin's concept of "survival of the fittest" to human society, believed that superior progeny could be bred by encouraging wealthier families to have more children while limiting the reproduction of the "unfit."

It was into this fertile new soil that Margaret Sanger, founder of Planned Parenthood, planted her new ideas. Many people accept this organization as providing needed, realistic counseling services to prevent unplanned births. It is less well known that its founder wrote articles such as the one that appeared in the November 1921 edition of *Birth Control Review,* entitled, "Birth Control: To Create a Race of Thoroughbreds."[8]

Sanger made such disturbing statements as, "The most

merciful thing that the large family does to one of its infant members is to kill it,"[9] and "the eugenicists wanted to shift the birth control emphasis from less children for the poor to more children for the rich. We went back and sought first to stop the multiplication of the unfit. This appeared the most important and greatest step towards race betterment."[10]

The eugenics movement and its underlying ideal of creating a "race of thoroughbreds" represented a great divergence from the teaching of most religions, which emphasized that every individual has immense intrinsic value whether they come from "unfit" parentage or not.

**U.S. faces birth dirth, *not* overpopulation**

Ironically, the developed countries in Europe and the United States where the Eugenics movement has been the strongest face a problem not of overpopulation, but of *underpopulation*. To replace itself, a population needs each woman to have 2.1 children over her lifetime to replace her and her mate, excluding immigration. Fifty-eight of the world's countries have less-than-replacement fertility rates. Five of these countries–Bulgaria, Italy, the Czech Republic, Romania and Spain– have a rate of 1.2 children per woman. Other countries, such as Germany, Japan, Greece, Russia, Portugal, Hungary, and the Ukraine, are only slightly higher.[11] In the year 2000, for the first time in history, people over 60 will outnumber kids 14 or younger in industrial countries.

For these countries, the fiscal consequences of these trends are severe. According to the Organization for Economic Cooperation and Development (OECD), over the next 25 years, the number of persons of pensionable age (65 and over) in industrial countries will rise by 70 million, while the working-age population will rise by only 5 million. Today, working taxpayers outnumber nonworking pensioners in the developed world by 3 to 1. By 2030, absent increases in retirement ages, this ratio will fall to 1.5 to 1.[12]

Who will pay the bills? One option would be to raise taxes on the diminishing number of workers. But according to official projections, doing so would require increasing the tax burden on workers by 25 to 40 percent of their taxable wages. Other options include cutting benefits or greatly increasing public debt.

In the United States, only 11 states have replacement-level populations. The rest have below-replacement fertility rates.[13] Underpopulation can lead to severe economic consequences including the projected underfunding of the Social Security and Medicare programs in the United States in decades to come. As in other countries, the declining number of new workers combined with a large aging population is a serious problem since Social Security taxes on present workers are used to support those who have already retired. One way to make up for low birth rates is to allow large numbers of immigrants into the United States, but this would create other challenges that must be addressed.

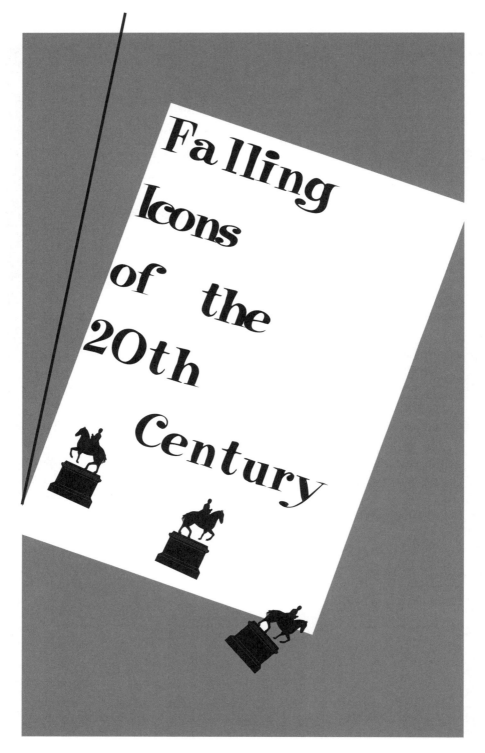

# Falling Icons of the 20th Century

# Margaret Mead  (1901-1978)

It was into this early 20th century cauldron of ideas that Margaret Mead burst with the 1928 publication of *Coming of Age in Samoa*. This book was published as scientific proof that unrestrained sex was not only not evil, but was the healthiest sex. The book received wild acceptance. She concluded, for example, that the exceptionally smooth sexual adjustment among adult Samoans is preceded by a time of free lovemaking and promiscuity before marriage by adolescents.[14]

As mentioned in the last chapter, Derek Freeman, Martin Orans, and other anthropologists have shown that Mead was deluded. She was a twenty-three year old graduate student who spent a mere nine months in Samoa; she did not live among the natives and she had a very poor grasp of the language. Her published findings were, at best, naive, and at worst, dishonest.

Because Mead's work was deemed by most opinionmakers to possess authority, it became a guide for proper childrearing and justification for sharing more sexual knowledge with children and a more permissive attitude toward childhood and adolescent sexual practice.[15]

# Sigmund Freud

Sigmund Freud

Dr. Sigmund Freud (1856-1939), the founder of psycho-analysis in the early part of the 20th century, had enormous impact not just in the field of psychology, but upon our entire culture. Freud believed that the sex drive, which he called "libido," was the primary human drive and that its repression was the root of all psychological problems and mental illness. By exploring early, formative events in one's childhood with a psychoanalyst, one could begin to understand oneself and gain some measure of freedom from the influence of unconscious motives and repressed memories.

The impact of Freud on 20th century culture cannot be overestimated. Sexual openness was now seen as the wave of the future. Sexual modesty was seen as repression, an old-fashioned relic from the Victorian age, and even hypocritical. Even though Freud never advocated sexual promiscuity,[16] mass culture took his theory of sexual repression to imply that sexual expression, whether inside or outside of marriage, is mentally healthy and good, whereas anything limiting it is mentally unhealthy, hypocritical and "repressed."

# Alfred Kinsey

Another challenge to traditional values regarding saving sex for marriage came from Dr. Alfred C. Kinsey (1894-1956). Kinsey was a zoologist at the University of Indiana, who turned his studies from gall wasps to the sexual behavior of male humans with the publication of *Sexual Behavior in the Human Male* (1948) and *Sexual Behavior in the Human Female* a few years later. In the first he claimed that detailed scientific research showed that 10% of men in the U.S. were homosexual, 70% of men had had sex with prostitutes, and that 30-45% of husbands had had extramarital affairs. He also claimed that children could achieve sexual orgasm from birth.[17]

While several experts challenged his research, the mass media was quick to embrace his titillating findings. It has since been clearly documented that Kinsey's research was far from objective or scientific, since 25% of the men he interviewed were prisoners or ex-convicts and 5% were male prostitutes. This sample was hardly representative of the American population.[18] In the *Female* report he claimed to have found that sexual abuse of young girls to be harmless, claiming that adult women were *never* traumatized by childhood sexual abuse and incest. His report also classified unmarried prostitutes and strippers in the "married" category.[19]

Many scientific studies show much lower rates of adulterous affairs by husbands than Kinsey stated.[20] Recent scientific surveys of men in the United States show that 1-2% are homosexual, not 10% as Kinsey alleged.[21, 22]

We now know that much of Kinsey's "scientific research" concerning the sexuality of children was based on the experiences of a single pedophile who had abused hundreds of boys and girls.[23] An excerpt from an article published in the *London Daily Telegraph* in August, 1998 follows:

*ALFRED Kinsey, the American sexologist whose ground-breaking Sexual Behaviour in the Human Male was published 50 years ago, based much of his "scientific research" on the experiences of a sole predatory paedophile, according to new evidence.*

*Kinsey, credited as the father of the Sexual Revolution, whose statistics and research ushered in the age of sexual liberation, based a key section of his book about the behaviour of children on the experiences of a man who had abused at least 800 boys and girls.*

*The man, an American government land examiner now named as Rex King, was given the code-name "Mr Green". He was contacted by Kinsey after he had heard that King had recorded in explicit detail his catalogue of abuse in a series of diaries, which he had buried in the Arizona desert.*

*Kinsey's reliance on a paedophile emerged a year ago with the publication of a biography, but the content of the diaries, recorded over a 20-year period, ...shows that Kinsey's chapter on the sexual behaviour of children was based solely on King's experiences, after the sexologist had convinced himself that they were "vital data." In 1948 Kinsey published large sections of "Mr Green's" diaries verbatim in his book but, rather than presenting them as the claims of a child abuser, he put them forward as the first scientific "proof" that children were sexual beings from birth. In what scientists now say totally discredits much of his research, [it has been learned that] Kinsey published - with no independent corroboration - Green's detailed descriptions of how he abused hundreds of children. Green lent his analysis a quasi-scientific bent by timing children's reactions with a stopwatch. Kinsey, who died in 1956, concluded that children could, with the assistance of an experienced adult, enjoy sexual activity from the moment they were born.[24]*

Despite the unscientific, unethical and illegal (child abuse) basis of his research and with the media's unquestioning promotion, Kinsey had an enormous impact in changing sexual norms–the public's views of what most Americans were doing sexually. His fraudulent research did much to break down societal values regarding reserving sex for marriage.

# Herbert Marcuse

*Herbert Marcuse gained world renown during the 1960s as a philosopher, social theorist, and political activist. As a University*

*professor and author of many books and articles, he won notoriety as a*
*defender of the "New Left" in the United States and Europe.*

*His theory of "one-dimensional" society criticized both Western*
*capitalist and state communist societies, but it was his book, Eros and*
*Civilization,*[25] which sought to synthesize Marxist theories of liberation with a Freudian understanding of the power and importance
of the sex drive. In *Eros and Civilization* he sketched the outlines of
a non-repressive civilization which would involve libidinal and
non-alienated labor, play, free and open sexuality, and production
of a society and culture which would further freedom and happiness. His utopian vision of sexual liberation anticipated many of
the values of the 1960s counterculture and gave them philosophical and "revolutionary" legitimacy.[26]

# Impact of Economic and Technological Changes on Sexual Behavior

The impact of thinkers such as Mead, Freud, Kinsey, Marcuse
and others claiming to represent the authority of science and the
"forces of history" was enormous, but these intellectual trends paralleled economic and technological changes affecting the family. In
the 19th and early 20th centuries, industrialization transformed a
largely agrarian society into a nation with many urban centers containing large numbers of factory workers and their families. On the
farm, mother, father, and children usually spent a lot of time with
each other and with an extended family who lived nearby. There
was a lot of work to do, and children were enlisted in the family
business at an early age.

With urbanization and mass production, fathers often had to
leave home to go work in a factory. Government-sponsored

schools were created to educate children and to prepare them to participate in an increasingly technological society. With increased opportunities for women to pursue careers, many children had less contact with their mothers as well. All these changes meant that children spent larger amounts of time away from their parents and other adult relatives.

The widespread distribution of radio programs and movies early in the 20th century and television in the 1950s transformed the culture profoundly. Prior to these mass media, most culture was local. Music, dance, and stories were passed down from generation to generation through families and neighbors. Values communicated through these cultural forms were generally the values of the local community.

In contrast, most of our cultural life is now defined by distant strangers. The family previously served as a screen for the child from the world, selecting what it deemed worthy of attention by the child. For children who are given large daily doses of television the family has decreasing impact on children's lives. Producers of popular music, movies, television talkshows, sitcoms, and soap operas may have little concern about what impact their shows have on children's lives.

Another history-altering event was the release of the first birth control pill by the Food and Drug Administration in 1960. The Pill offered a promise of sexual freedom without the consequence of pregnancy.

It took a magazine publisher named Hugh Hefner to popularize the "free sex" ideas of the free thinkers using developments in color printing technology. He helped usher in a multi-billion dollar industry that makes money by marketing uncommitted sex.

## Hugh Hefner

Hugh Hefner (Born1926) was the founder of *Playboy* magazine, first published in 1953. He brought the Sexual Revolution and soft pornography into the living rooms of America. Deeply inspired by Kinsey, Hefner sought to redefine manhood and womanhood. In his view, a man to admire is one who cultivates his pursuit of pleasure, including having sex with many partners. Such a man is a connoisseur of fine wines, fast cars, and beautiful women.

Hefner believed that women should be able to sell sex and men should be able to buy it. Sex is something to be freely sold in the sexual marketplace, not something to be reserved for one person in the context of a marriage vow.

We now know that the swinging singles who conform to the Playboy model are not more sexually fulfilled. Those with multiple partners are the least likely to be sexually fulfilled when compared to those who are faithful to one lifelong partner.[27] In fact, Hefner himself married in 1989 (for the second time), perhaps realizing that the life of a swinging single is not as exciting as his highly profitable magazine, and all its clones make it out to be.[28] In 1998, Hefner and his second wife separated.

# Post-World War II | Feminism

The feminist movement in the early part of the 20th century focused on winning women the right to vote and expanding educational and career opportunities. In the 1950s and 1960s feminist writers like Simone de Beauvoir and Betty Friedan began to realize that even if there were expanded opportunities, most women were unlikely to pursue jobs and careers outside the home without a stronger critique of marriage and home life. In *The Second Sex*, de Beauvoir portrayed marriage and family life as an oppressive institution women would be better off escaping from.[29] In *The Feminine Mystique*, Betty Friedan described the restlessness and malaise of women who lacked opportunities for personal growth and development. Their personal growth, she suggested, depended on finding paid work outside the home.[30]

In 1972, an influential book by sociologist Jessie Bernard, *The Future of Marriage*, took the position that marriage was good for men and bad for women. Compared with unmarried women, Bernard claimed, married women were more likely to suffer mental and physical problems and that for a woman to be happy in a traditional marriage, "a woman must be slightly ill mentally." She did not propose a reform of marriage to make it equal and mutually fulfilling for both husband and wife. Rather her solution envisioned a "future of options"--a social situation in which the institution of marriage was one of many options ranging from celibacy, trial marriage, open marriage, group marriage, nonsexual marriage, cohabitation, and singleness with an active sexual life.[31]

As we have seen, Jessie Bernard's belief that "marriage is bad for women" is false, yet it fit in perfectly with the views of many influential sociologists and feminists, sometimes called "gender feminists," that marriage as an oppressive institution of male dominance and "patriarchal power."

Gender feminists had an enormous impact throughout the academic world, but especially in the field of Sociology. Advocates of "family pluralism" argued that the traditional two-parent family is just one of many choices of "kinship preferences." Judith Stacey, a professor of Sociology at Cal State, writes in her 1996 book, *In the Name of the Family:* "It is time to lay to rest the ghost of The Family so that we may begin to build a safe world for living families. The Family is dead. Long live our families!"[32]

In an earlier book, *Brave New Families*, Stacey declared, "The 'family' is not here to stay. Nor should we wish it were...all democratic people, whatever their kinship preferences, should work to hasten its demise." In other words, if you believe in democratic values, you should work to abolish marriage and the two-parent family as a recommended norm.[33]

## Postmodernism, the New Historicism, and the Radical Questioning of Gender

In the late 20th century, in reaction to the technological optimism (and some would say, arrogance) and austere and, often, abstract forms of modernism in architecture, arts, literature and culture, *postmodern* culture undertook an eclectic, often ironic, approach characterized by the rejection of absolutes in style and even in the idea of truth itself. If John Wayne or Jimmy Stewart fightng against bad guy x, y, or z with a Donna Reed type at his side incarnated the black and white hues of popular culture for the WWII generation, who embodies the postmodern age? Woody Allen, Jerry Seinfeld, Courtney Love? When truth itself is in question, is there anything worth fighting for?

Michel Foucault (1926-1984), professor of the History of Systems of Thought at the College of France beginning in 1970 launched what some call the New Historicism through such influential works as *Madness and Civilization (1961), The Order of Things (1966)* and *The History of Sexuality (1976-84).* In these works Foucault argued that power and social control are exercised not just through physical coercion, but in myriads of ways including the structure of language itself and the categorizing of "normalcy" and "perversion."[34] Foucault laid the foundation for a radical questioning by "gender feminists" and "queer theorists" of gender, the idea of essential masculine and femine natures.

They argued that far from being rooted in biology, male and female roles are social constructs that are essentially artificial and used to exert rigid social control. For this reason, feminist and queer theorists often celebrate gender nonconformists (gay men, lesbians, bisexuals, transsexuals, transvestites and 'gender-disordered' children) because they challenge the two-gender model.

Judith Lorber, author of *Paradoxes of Gender* (Yale University Press), lists five sexes on the basis of genitalia; three sexual orientations based on object choice (heterosexual, homosexual, or bisexual); five gender displays; six types of emotional bonds; ten to fourteen kinds of sexual identifications; and an uncountable number of sexual practices.[35] These academic trends have impacted the thinking of a sizable number of students and faculty alike. One recent graduate from an elite liberal arts college explains how her professor said to her with pity, "you're just an essentialist," a putdown describing someone who believes in inherent human nature or, "even worse," absolute truth.

## Classic Case Shows Sexual Identity Not Pliable After All

A classic case involving a gruesome surgical accident and its consequences has long been used as evidence of the malleability of sexual identity and gender. In 1973, researchers at Johns Hopkins University in Baltimore reported the account of an infant boy whose penis had been accidently cut off and who was subsequently reared as a girl. The child appeared to have accepted the new identity and to be happy with life as a girl.

The case became famous and entered the textbooks as proof that infants are "more or less sexually neutral at birth, establishing sexual identification only with socialization and exposure to the binary world of boys and girls, blue and pink, guns and Barbies."[36]

More than twenty years later, two researchers presented an in-depth follow-up that refuted the initial reports of a glowing success. Their report, which appeared in the *Archives of Pediatric and Adolescent Medicine*, found that far from being satisfied with his reassignment to girlhood, the boy renounced his female identity at the age of fourteen and chose to live as a man, even undergoing extensive surgery to attempt a reconstruction of his genitals.

In 1997, when he was in his thirties, the patient was married and found to be as well-adjusted as could be expected of one who had been through such an ordeal. "Despite everyone telling him constantly that he was a girl, and despite his being treated with female hormones, his brain knew he was a male. It refused to take on what it was being told," said Dr. William Reiner of Johns Hopkins Hospital in an interview reported in the *New York Times*.[37]

# College Textbooks on Marriage

When we look at college textbooks on marriage, we often see an unrelenting bias against marriage. A textbook called *Changing Families* by Judy Root Aulette devotes three chapters to marriage: "Battering and Marital Rape," "Divorce and Remarriage," and "Marriage." None point out any of marriage's benefits.

Aulette incorrectly states that "marriage is an institution that exists in some societies but not in others." In fact, marriage appears again and again in every known human society. She argues that "the idea and practice of monogamous marriage must have been created for the first time at some 'specific' moment in history," citing Friedrich Engels, coauthor with Karl Marx of the Communist Manifesto in 1848. Engels believed that "marriage was created for a particular purpose: *to control women and children*."[38]

Marxism-Leninism, the ideology which led to the creation of Communist "dictatorships of the proletariat," is now nearly extinct all over the world, but is *alive and well* in several American college textbooks on the family. Aulette is honest about the origins of her feminist analysis: "Engels proposed that marriage was originally designed to facilitate both maintenance of class inequality and the oppression of women. *His ideas have been criticized by radical, social-ist, and Marxist feminists but the central argument he makes about the connection of marriage and the oppression of women is one upon which they agree.*[39] (italics added for emphasis)

While other college textbooks on marriage are less ideologically extreme, nearly all neglect to discuss the benefits of marriage in any depth. Some don't mention marriage favorably at all. A report by the *Council on Families,* called "Closed Hearts, Closed Minds: The Textbook Story of Marriage," found that of twenty textbooks analyzed, "five of them have no treatment at all of marital effects on well-being. Five others devote from one sentence to less than one page to the topic. No book devotes more than 3.5 pages to the topic; the average was 1.25 pages."[40]

It is common to hear people rage against trends toward censorship in America. Where is the rage at the bias against and censorship of discussions of the benefits of marriage? America's college students will be many of our country's future teachers, counselors, TV writers, directors and producers, social workers, lawyers, judges, policymakers, elected leaders and fathers and mothers. Don't they deserve to hear a more balanced discussion?

## Popular Culture
## Women's Pornography and the Internet

If the gender feminist bias against marriage were limited to college textbooks, it is unlikely it would impact the lives of most Americans. But the reality is that the private sector is more than willing to bombard us with anti-marriage, pro-adultery messages.

In the '50s and '60s, popular music became more explicitly sexual. Elvis' rotating pelvis scandalized parents and captivated their kids. Rock n' Roll, a term which originally referred to the act of sexual intercourse, spread across the land. While many rock song lyrics were about love and even marriage, an increasing number were admittedly more on the "lust" side. Helen Gurley Brown, the founder and editor-in-chief of *Cosmopolitan* magazine, popularized the realm of "women's pornography." Unlike men's pornography, the core of which is pictures of naked women, most "women's pornography" consists not of pictures of nude men, but of romantic fantasies about steamy, always sensual uncommitted sex.

In TV-land, it's hard to find fathers who are dedicated, involved and competent. A 1999 study by the National Fatherhood Initiative (NFI) found that out of 102 prime-time TV shows on television networks including NBC, CBS, ABC, Fox and Warner Brothers, only 15, or 14.7%, had fathers as regular, central characters. Only 4 of the 15 shows which had fathers as recurring central characters had "positive" characterizations in which the TV fathers are involved with their children, offer moral guidance, are competent as fathers and make the family a priority. In fact, NFI points out, if you were to pick a TV show at random, it is at least *fifteen times more likely* that you will be watching a show where sex between unmarried adults is the recurrent and central theme than a show where responsible fatherhood is a recurring and central feature.

According to Wade Horn, President of the National Fatherhood Initiative, the four shows with the worst dads were WB's "Dawson's Creek," Fox's "That '70s Show," ABC's "Brother's Keeper," and CBS' "The Nanny," which scored the lowest on the responsible dad scale. The top father figures are Stephen Collins' the Rev. Eric Camden on WB's "7th Heaven" and Gerald McRaney's Russell Greene in CBS' "Promised Land." The other good dads are in WB's "Smart Guy" and ABC's "Two of a Kind," NFI said. NBC had only one father as a recurring central character on its entire prime time schedule, Paul Reiser's character on *Mad About You*. No prime-time shows on Saturday night had a recurring father figure, even though that was when families were likely to watch TV together.[42]

A book Brown wrote in the early 1960s, *Sex and the Single Girl*, makes the agenda clear. Brown explained that not only was it okay for single women to have sex outside of marriage, but they were *entitled to it as an issue of equality*.[41] Her solution to the historical doublestandard? Get rid of the standard, period.

The reality that women pay the highest price for uncommitted sex through single parenthood, higher rates of depression and sickness, violent victimization, and poverty are details that magazines like *Cosmopolitan* conveniently ignore.

Cultural idols like Madonna, 'Gangsta' Rappers, and others have profited mightily from challenging old taboos against having sex outside of marriage. Such superstars can gain fame and notoriety as "rebels" while multibillion dollar companies market their songs all over the globe. Not very admirable when you realize that the marketing of uncommitted sex leads to millions of fatherless children.

Some young people have never known a world in which uncommitted sex wasn't marketed constantly over the airwaves, on MTV, and on the Internet. Consequently they think that sexualized world is just the way things have always been and always will be. Of course, our sexualized culture is not an act of nature–it is the conscious creation of *individuals* with the backing of corporations with strong appetites, for profits.

[1] Following discussion draws from address by Joe S. McIlhaney, Jr., M. D. at the Oklahoma Governor's Conference on Abstinence, September 1998.

[2] Genesis 2:2

[3] Song of Solomon 5:1.

4 B. Gottlieb, *The Family in the Western World: from the Black Death to the Industrial Age*, New York, Oxford, 1993, 99.

[5] A. Powell, *Living Buddhism*, Berkeley: Univ. of California Press, 1995, 24. Also, The *Dalai Lama: The Power of Compassion*, San Francisco: Thorson, 1995, 59.

[6] D. Kinsley, *Hinduism: a Cultural Perspective*, Englewood Cliffs, NJ: Prentice

A Kaiser Family Foundation study found that three out of four shows on network TV during "family hour" contained sexual behavior or verbal references to sex. The study, "Sex, Kids and the Family Hour," found that in each hour of family programming between 8 to 9 pm, there were an average of 8.5 incidents of sexual behavior, with little or no information about the risks or responsibilities of such behavior. 75% of family hour programs contain some sexual content-either talk about sex or behavior. Twenty years earlier, in the 1970s, 43% of programming had such content. Children in a focus group indicated that sexual content does not "go over their heads," researchers said. Only 6% of shows with sexual content emphasized sexual risks and responsibilities.[43]

The usual explanation for our media being in heat is that sex sells. If only it were that simple. Michael Medved, the film and culture critic, and others have pointed out that "G" and "PG" rated films make much more profit on average than do ubiquitous "R" rated films. In his book, *Hollywood versus America*, Medved pointed out that in a ten year period, in *Variety's* list of the Top 10 box-office films, only one was an "R" film, even though "R" films accounted for more than 60% of all titles released during that time period. At the same time, "PG" films represented less than 25% of all titles-but occupied *six* of the Top 10 places on the list of the decade's leading money-makers. An analysis of 1,010 domestic releases found that all "G" films achieved a median box office gross of $17.3 million, while "PG" titles achieved a median figure of $13.0 million. "R" pictures returned a pathetic median gross of $8.3 million.[44]

What Hollywood media moguls seek apparently is not so much the almighty dollar, but the admiration of their peers in the media industry. A *U.S. New & World Report* survey found that while 80% of the Americans expressed concern about references to sex, nudity, and premarital and extramarital sex on TV, half as many Hollywood executives were upset by these. Even higher percentages of the public said that television portrayals of sex contributed to casual, premarital, extramarital and teen sex.[45] Despite the billions of advertizing dollars spent on TV commercials, few Hollywood executives thought television had any impact on behavior in this area.

Hall, 1993. Also, V.P. Kantikar and O. Cole, *Teach Yourself Hinduism,* Chicago, NTC Publishing Group, 1995, 84.

7 G. Brooks, *Nine Parts of Desire: The Hidden World of Islamic Women,* New York, Anchor Hardcover, 1995, 39.

8 "Unity!", *Birth Control Review,* November 1921, vol. 5, no. 11, p. 3

9 Margaret Sanger , *Women and the New Race,* 62-63, as discussed in Douglas Scott's *Bad Choices: a Look Inside Planned Parenthood,* Legacy Communications, Franklin, TN, 1992.

10 Margaret Sanger, *Margaret Sanger: an Autobiography,* 374-5, as discussed in Douglas Scott's *Bad Choices: a Look Inside Planned Parenthood,* Legacy Communications, Franklin, TN, 1992.

11 Cheryl Wetzstein, "Fertility rates drop in U.S., other developed nations," *The Washington Times Weekly National Edition,* February 15-21, 1999.

12 Philip Longman, "The World Turns Gray: How global aging will challenge the world's economic well-being," *U.S. News & World Report,* March 1, 1999, 30-39.

13 National Center for Health Statistics.

14 D. Freeman, *Margaret Mead and Samoa: the Making and Unmaking of an Anthropological Myth,* Cambridge, MA: Harvard University Press, 1983.

15 M. Orans, *Not Even Wrong: Margaret Mead, Derek Freeman, and the Samoans,* Novato, CA: Chandler and Sharp, 1996.

16 Sigmund Freud, *Civilization and its Discontents,* 1930, 54.

17 Alfred C. Kinsey, Wardell B. Pomeroy, and Clyde E. Martin, *Sexual Behavior in the Human Male,* W. B. Saunders, Philadelphia, 1948.

18 Judith A. Reisman and Edward W. Eichel, *Kinsey, Sex and Fraud: The Indoctrination of a People,* Huntington House, Lafayette, LA, 1990. James H. Jones, *Alfred C. Kinsey, a Public/Private Life,* Norton and Company, New York, 1997.

19 Judith A. Reisman, Ph.D., *KINSEY: Crimes and Consequences,* Institute for Media Education, Arlington, VA, 1998, 110-139.

20 Robert T. Michael et al, *Sex in America: a definitive study,* Little, Brown, and Co., New York, 1994. Michael and others working with the National Opinion Research Center (NORC) found that about 20% of married men had cheated on their wives, much lower than Kinsey's findings about men living at a more conservative time . The NORC study is considered much more scientific because a large number of people were interviewed, because the people interviewed were chosen at random and a high percentage of those chosen completed the indepth interview. Other studies show similar results.

21 Boyce Rensberger, "2.3% in survey report homosexual encounter," *Washington Post News Service,* April 15, 1993.

22 Felicity Barringer, "Sex Survey of American Men Finds 1% Are Gay," *New York Times,* April 15, 1993. "The Sexual Behavior of Men in the United States," *Family Planning Perspectives,* April 15, 1993, Alan Guttmacher Institute, New York.

23 Reisman, *KINSEY: Crimes and Consequences,* op cit., 140-170.

24 Tim Reid, "Kinsey based research on child abuser," *London Daily*

*Telegraph*, August 9, 1998.

25 Herbert Marcuse, *Eros and Civilization*, Boston: Beacon Press, 1955

26 "Herbert Marcuse" by Douglas Kellner, www.uta.edu/huma/illumina-tions/kell12.htm

27 Robert T. Michael, op cit.

28 "Hugh M. Hefner, Biography," from the PLAYBOY.COM website, Playboy Enterprises, 1998.

29 Simone de Beauvoir, *The Second Sex*, New York, Knopf, 1953.

30 Betty Friedan, *The Feminine Mystique*, New York, Dell, 1964.

31 Jessie Bernard, Ph.D., *The Future of Marriage*, New York, World Publishing, 1972, 51.

32 Judith Stacey, *In the Name of the Family: Rethinking Family Values in the Postmodern Age*, Beacon Press, Boston, 1996.

33 Judith Stacey, *Brave New Families*, Basic Books, New York, 1990.

34 For a detailed discussion of Foucault's, and other's,thoughts on erasing the boundary between sexual normalcy and perversion, especially with reference to the writings of Marquis de Sade, now a popular mainstay in many college cur-ricula and academic conferences, read Roger Shattuck's *Forbidden Knowledge: from Prometheus to Pornography*, St. Martin's Press, New York, 1996. As our language now suggests, Marquis de Sade was the lyricist for the joys of sadistic sex, incest, sexual abuse of children, torture and murder. He spent decades in prison for many of these crimes.

35 Alan Wolfe, "The Gender Question: Women and men in the mirror of feminist theory," *The New Republic*, Vol. 210, No. 23, Issue 4, June 6, 1994, Washington, D.C

36 Natalie Angier, "Sexual Identity Not Pliable After All, Report Says, *New York Times*, March 14, 1997, A1.

37 Ibid.

38 Judy Root Aulette, *Changing Families*, Wadsworth, Belmont, CA, 1994, 273

.39 Ibid., 278.

40 Norval Glenn, "Closed Hearts, Closed Minds: The Textbook Story of Marriage," *Institute for American Values*, New York, 1997.

41 Helen Gurley Brown, *Sex and the Single Girl*, B. Geis and Associates, dis-tributed by Random House, 1962.

42 "Fatherhood and TV: What Does Prime Time Network Television Say About Fatherhood, *National Fatherhood Initiative*, Gaithersburg, Maryland, March, 1999.

43 Annie Nakao, "Sexual references seen multiplying in TV 'family hour,'" San Francisco Examiner, December 21, 1996.

44 Michael Medved, *Hollywood vs. America: popular culture and the war on tra-ditional values*, HarperCollins, New York, 1992, 287.

45 Linda Chavez, "Hollywood misses American reality," *USA Today*, May, 1996.

# chapter five

# AFTER THE Sexual Revolution

# How Did Men Respond to the Feminist and Sexual Revolutions?

The majority of unmarried young men have always been ready to pursue premarital sex. After all, it is women who have always paid the highest price for uncommitted sex. Most cultures tacitly accept a double standard, saying that "men will be men." In some cultures, men even take their 12-year-old sons to prostitutes to initiate them into "manhood."

What was different about the Feminist/Sexual Revolutions that took place in the second half of the 20th Century was that they successfully convinced many *women* to accept and pursue uncommitted sex. After all, if most *women* aren't willing to accept extramarital sex, there is no "revolution." Most men will follow what the majority of women insist upon. But if women are unclear about their standards, or even actively pursue uncommitted sex,

many men will be more than happy to go along.

Feminist writers such as Naomi Wolf wrote about the need for women to liberate the "shadow slut" within. They seem to see female sexual freedom as a way for women to escape age-old restrictions and as a way to exert power over men. Indeed, it can be said that an attractive sexually active woman can achieve considerable power over many, if not all, men. But then the question becomes who is controlling whom?

"OUR IDEAS WERE ADOPTED AND ADAPTED INTO THE COUNTERCULTURE OF THE '60s, THE PROTESTS OF THE ANTIWAR MOVEMENT (REMEMBER 'MAKE LOVE, NOT WAR'? — HAVING BIRTH CONTROL PILLS AROUND HELPED — USUALLY) TIMOTHY LEARY ('TURN ON AND DROP OUT'), THE GRATEFUL DEAD, AND, YES, THE HIPPIES."

Make Love ♥ Not War

After a succession of affairs many women begin to realize that their biological clock is ticking and that they really do want to have a marriage and children. Popular TV shows like HBO's "Sex and the City" deal with the ambivalence of attractive single women who have ample access to uncommitted sex. And do women really want to become as predatory as the most egoistic of men? Of course, many women see sexual expression not as a Machiavellian exercise in power but simply as a way to explore the crevices of human desire and the yearnings of their hearts. But reality has a way of cutting fantasy and even whirlpools of desire down to size.

It is tragically ironic that the Feminist/Sexual Revolution gave carte blanche to the most immature male libidos (in a codependent alliance with female fantasy). You didn't have to twist the arms of most men to go along with *this item* on the feminist agenda. Many men effectively said, "You feminists want to allow women sexual freedom equal to men's? You want to abolish patriarchy through consensual sex with no strings attached? Sign me up! I'm a feminist!"

As suggested by Marcuse, hopping into bed became a revolutionary act, or at least socially acceptable. "Make love, not war!" was more than an idealistic anti-war slogan during the '60s and '70s. Of course, when women came back and said, "I'm pregnant," the reaction of many men was, "You agreed to have sex with no

strings attached. You wanted to be free from any commitments. This is *your problem*, not mine."

Ironically, feminist leaders like Gloria Steinem[1] reinforced these selfish male attitudes by making statements like, "A woman without a man is like a fish without a bicycle." The feminist attack on traditional masculine roles of husband and father undermined the social sanction for the traditional male role of supporting a family. In other words, men could act callously with less and less social penalty. In other words, they didn't have to grow up.

The number of men who considered providing for a family and children a vital life goal dropped by 50% from the 1950s to the 1970s.[2] The combination of feminist ideology and male irresponsibility disenfranchised millions of children. Of course, at the dawn of the 21st century, "make love, not war" is no longer seen by anyone as a revolutionary act. For many, it's just the way things have always been.

As the connection between the initiation of intimacy and marriage became more blurry, the meaning and importance of marriage itself came into question. Increasing numbers of men and especially women became convinced that the best solution to marital unhappiness was to "bail out." With nearly every state in the Union following California in passing "no-fault" divorce, the marriage contract could be *unilaterally revoked by one spouse* under the catch-all of "irreconcilable differences."

Laws enforcing payments from "deadbeat dads" have been less than successful in getting men to support their children. Even when they do, it is more often much less than was given voluntarily before the divorce. Men were effectively told by both the law and society: "you are totally unnecessary for this family, *except for your paycheck."* Such an atmosphere is not conducive to generosity.

Previous concerns about the impact of divorce upon children were replaced with concern about the feelings of the spouse demanding the divorce. Adults were now seen as extremely fragile, but children could be expected to make all kinds of adjustments. Children were expected to tough it out and "get over it." Divorcees were comforted by a plethora of books like one written by Mel Krantzler, author of *Creative Divorce: A New Opportunity for Personal Growth.* This book optimistically stated: "Children can survive any family crisis without permanent damage-and grow as human beings in the process."[3]

Hollywood played to the prevailing cynicism about marriage by producing such movies as *The Graduate,* which portrayed American parents as cynical and materialistic and included the uplifting scene of Mrs. Robinson seducing her daughter's college boyfriend. With rare exceptions, in Hollywood's eyes, good marriages either didn't exist or were so devoid of dramatic potential they weren't worth exploring.

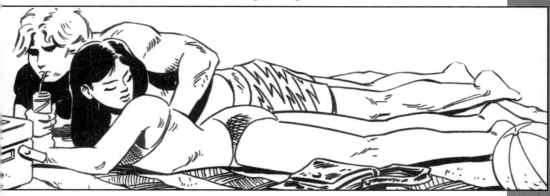

# Explosions in Divorce
# & Out-of-Wedlock Births

The explosion in divorce took full force in the 1970s. Divorce rates doubled. One in 5 children born in the '70s saw their parents divorce or separate by the time they reached age 18.[4] In the 1990s, a million American children experienced the divorce or separation of their parents *each year.*[5]

In 1998, about 20 million children under 18 years of age in the

United States lived with just one parent, representing 28 percent of children. In addition, another 4 million children, nearly 6 percent of all children under 18, lived in the household of their grandparents, indicating that they missed the love and attention of not just one parent, but two.[6] Of course, these 4 million kids were lucky to have grandparents willing to take care of them. The alternative usually is to be cycled through foster homes.

With adults rejecting traditional standards of reserving sex for marriage, many teenagers wanted to get in on the fun. When teens asked, "Why not?" many adults couldn't give an answer. When boyfriends came around, parents often looked the other way or simply weren't around to say anything. Reflecting these changes in attitudes, 3 in 4 participants in a survey by *Child Trends* said it's okay for single women to have babies outside of marriage.[7] Governments stopped enforcing statutory rape laws. Many girls became pregnant. Because of their immaturity, they were unable to take care of or support their children.

This teen sexual revolution exposed younger teenage girls in particular to predatory sex with older male teens and even grown men. One national survey found that half of the "fathers" (egg-fertilizers) of babies born to teen girls between the ages of 15 to 17 were 20 or older. Twenty percent of the fathers were six or more years older than the girl.[8] Another study reported that fathers are on average 9.8 years older than mothers 11 to 12 years of age; 4.6 years older than mothers 13 to 14 years of age; and 3.7 years older than mothers 15 to 19 years of age.[9] When men are driven out of the marriage bed and home, it leaves children, particularly girls, more vulnerable to sexual exploitation by older males.

A federal welfare program, Aid to Families with Dependent Children (AFDC), gave monthly financial support to single mothers, as long as there was no man officially living in the house. And if there is no one man in the house, the likelihood of a succession of *men* visiting the house for sexual trysts greatly increases. In a perverse way, this government policy provided incentives to teenage girls and young women to have children out-of-wedlock. Some argue that it would be unfair to say that unwed pregnancies and the decline of marriage in inner city neighborhoods were *caused by* government welfare policies, but this detrimental government policy certainly did nothing to *discourage* self-destructive sexual behavior. The absence of married husbands left the door

open for a succession of male visitors to create additional fatherless children.

It's one thing for Madonna, Jodie Foster, and other multi-
millionaire celebrities to have children out-of-wedlock. When you
are *that* wealthy you can hire nannies, cooks, and security guards
to take care of your children while you pursue a career, but when
you're at the bottom of the economic scale, the glamour is harder
to see. Of course, teen girls who never had a father around to
show them the masculine love they deserved are more likely to
seek love in the form of a sexually demanding older boyfriend.
When they are abandoned by the boyfriend/inseminator, as happens in the vast majority of cases, at least they have one or more
babies who they think will love them.

The explosion in uncommitted teen and adult sex in the U.S.
led to a 500% increase in out-of-wedlock births. The rates of
unmarried births among African-Americans rose to 70%, devastating their communities. The rates of illegitimacy among white
mothers more than tripled, rising to more than 25% by the mid
1990s.[10]

# Fatherless Families, Abandoned Children

Enthusiasts of "family pluralism" claimed that after divorce
ex-husbands or never-married male inseminators could continue
to fulfill the fatherhood role. Does that happen often? The *National
Survey of Children* found that in disrupted families only one child

in six saw his or her father every week in the previous year. Almost half didn't see their fathers *even once.*

The children who get to see their fathers once a week are the lucky ones. But what is a father? Is a father someone who takes you on a date once a week? Or is a father someone who gives you love, guidance–and, yes, discipline–on a daily basis? A whole new line of divorce cards was developed in Hallmark stores for guilty fathers to send to children they hadn't seen in a long time. The children who received those crumbs of love every few months were *the lucky ones.* Nearly half receive–no communication at all.

Advocates of "family pluralism" suggested that the mother's new boyfriends might fill in as substitute fathers. Sometimes that does indeed happen. Boys are especially hungry for older male companionship and guidance. Of course, when mom's boyfriend goes on to greener pastures, the children experience a new abandonment.

The movie *Jerry Maguire* about the on-and-off-again love affair/marriage between a high-powered sports agent played by Tom Cruise trying to follow his newly emerging conscience and a single mother with a ten year-old boy poignantly dealt with these themes. The single mother desperately wants a lasting love relationship, but constantly fears that, if the relationship breaks up, her son will suffer rejection again.

The struggle of the Tom Cruise/sports agent character between the poles of love/commitment versus "choice" and "emotional freedom" is an ongoing struggle for millions of American families. Jerry Maguire finally learns a lesson in fidelity from an otherwise flaky football player who happens to love his wife to pieces. Maguire finally decides to return to his wife. The wife's circle of resentful, man-hating women friends cannot believe their eyes–*a faithful, committed man!* They all burst into rapturous applause. Too bad this feel-good ending happens so seldom in real life. But the enormous popularity of this movie showed that it touched a deep nerve in the American psyche.

The children of divorce or the never-married suffer not just the withdrawal of emotional and financial support from their on-and-off-again fathers, but also from their mothers. Mothers who choose to, or are forced to, go to a job often have less time, energy, and resources to devote to their children. More often than not, there is no one at home to watch these children after school. If the mother wants to have any type of social life, her children may lose more of her time and attention.

Despite the spending of more than three *trillion* dollars in federal anti-poverty programs since the 1960s, poverty has persisted and even increased in the United States. But this is largely in female-headed households with no man around. While some women, particularly educated, upper middle-class women, may feel they have benefitted in various ways from the expansion of choice and opportunities through the greater freedom to divorce or to have a child without being married to the father, the sad reality is that *many* women experienced more misery and poverty as society turned away from a clear standard about marriage and parental responsibility. And how do we weigh social approval for a woman's right to have a child outside of marriage against the *child's* desire to know his or her father? That we even have to ask the question shows how far we've come in the direction of adult self-absorption.

According to the National *Kids Count Report* there are three virtual guarantees of child poverty in the U.S.: 1) birth outside of marriage, 2) a mother who was a teenager when she had her first child, 3) a mother who did not finish high school. Nearly 8 out of 10 children with these 3 risk factors live in poverty in the U.S., whereas those with none of these risk factors are 10 times less likely to live in poverty.[11]

If we truly care about the well-being of children, we have to be concerned about family structure. Only 1 in 10 children living with both natural parents live in poverty in the U.S. That increases to 4 in 10 living in poverty among the children of divorce. Poverty jumps to nearly 7 out of 10 for children whose parents never married. Remarriage reduces child poverty rates to 1 in 7.[12] (see chart on page 108)

When we look at the African-American community, the positive economic impact of marriage is especially clear: only 1

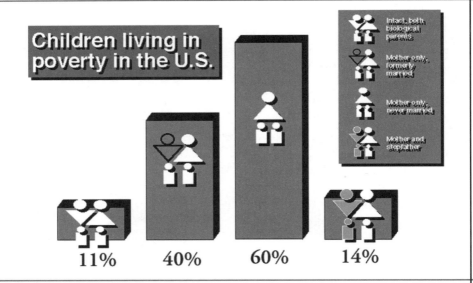

## Children living in poverty in the U.S.

Intact, both biological parents — 11%

Mother only, formerly married — 40%

Mother only, never married — 60%

Mother and stepfather — 14%

in 7 black children living with their married parents are poor compared to 6 in 10 of those living with their mother alone.[13]

Remarriage may help economically, but living in a stepfamily can be a difficult challenge. Treatment for emotional and behavioral problems are 3 times higher among children in step-families and 2 times higher among the children after a divorce compared to children living with both natural parents.[14] The children of divorce often struggle with feelings of abandonment or guilt because many children fear they may have contributed or even caused the divorce. Despite optimistic TV shows like the Brady Bunch, many children do not easily accept the new wife as their mother or a new husband as their father.

When the new husband tries to enforce discipline they often say, "Who are you to tell me what to do? You're not my father."

The rates of child abuse among children living in stepfamilies are shockingly high. As mentioned in the last chapter, one study showed that preschool children in such families were 40 times more likely to suffer physical or sexual abuse than children living with their original parents.[15] The reason is that the new husband doesn't automatically view his wife's children as *his children* and may find it difficult to summon forth the same love he would more naturally feel towards his own biological children. He may feel sexually attracted to his new wife's daughters.

California psychologist Judith Wallerstein began studying the long-term effects of divorce on children in the 1970s. As a supporter of no-fault divorce at the time, she expected to find that the effects on children would be more or less temporary. When she interviewed children a year after the divorce, she was surprised to find many children were still very troubled and obsessed with seeing their parents get back together.

She wrote of an interview with a five year-old named Sammy who more than one year after his parents' divorce still could not accept it. She asked Sammy, "If you had three wishes, Sammy, what would they be?" The little boy responded, in tears, "I wish they'd get back together. That's wish one, two, and three!" Bursting into a torrent of tears, he cried, "That's all that I want!"[16]

Think about what the average 5-year-old might wish for: a new game or toy. This 5-year-old's childhood world had been stolen from him. All he could think was: *I wish my parents were back together.*

Wallerstein found that 5 years after divorce, *more than a third* of the children still experienced depression. Ten years after divorce, a significant number were still troubled, drifting, and underachieving.[17]

An interview with a college student named Tanya, nearly 15 years after her parents divorce, revealed the persisting inner turmoil. Tanya asked Dr. Wallerstein about her own parents: "Did they ever love each other? Did they ever hug and make up after

# "Did they ever love each other? Did they ever hug and make up after they fought?"

they fought?" Without a good memory of parents who could love each other, she doubted that she could establish a loving relationship with a man..

In fact, children of divorce are more likely to have a succession of short-term relationships and to divorce themselves if they do get married. They haven't seen a successful model of a couple that goes beyond the inevitable conflicts. They learn that love *can't last*.

Pat Conroy, the novelist, wrote about his own divorce: "Each divorce is the death of a small civilization."[18] Every family, even those which are less than ideal, is a whole world of shared experiences and traditions. Divorce shatters shared dreams and also gives shared memories a gnawing, bitter aftertaste of pain. Since children are the result of and blending of both parents, when they split, it is as if the children themselves are being torn in half.

In 1994 the American Academy of Pediatrics revised its earlier optimism about the short-term effects of divorce on children. Up to half of children were likely to report such symptoms as aggression in school in school-age boys and depression in early and mid-adolescent girls. The Academy stated that divorce-related problems are likely to persist. Children's "sense of loss is ongoing and may reemerge especially on holidays, birthdays, special school events, and when attempting to integrate multiple new family relationships."[19]

The point here is not to point fingers or to accuse stepfamilies or fatherless families. Many of these are doing their best. *Many children living in such families will turn out fine*, despite the

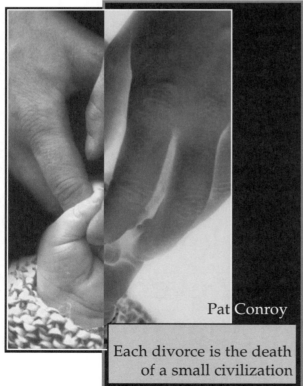

Pat Conroy

Each divorce is the death of a small civilization

emotional challenges they face. It's obvious that children living with their natural, married parents are not guaranteed heaven on earth. However, if we truly want to help children and to avoid increasing future misery for them, we have to look at these higher risk factors honestly.

Family stability also has a significant impact on academic achievement in schools. Two measures of this are the number of students who are forced to repeat a grade or who have been expelled or suspended from school. Rates for these are 2 times higher in divorced and step families and 3 times higher in families headed by women who have never been married.[20] (chart below) One of the things that fathers do is to encourage and challenge their kids, especially sons, to do well in school. Stepfathers may try to do this, but their bond with a stepchild and consequent authority are not nearly as much as that of natural fathers living in the same home.

Research also shows that children in non-intact families are much more likely to use cigarettes, alcohol, marijuana and other drugs. Girls are especially more likely to engage in teen sex. These differences are not diminished when you consider other factors such as the age, race, or educational level of the mother.[21]

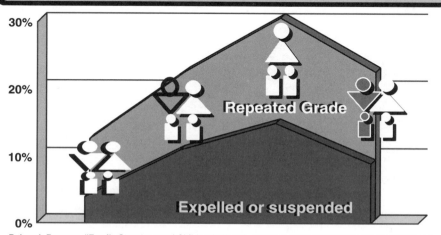

**Family structure and school performance**

Repeated Grade

Expelled or suspended

Deborah Dawson, "Family Structure and Children's Health and Well-Being: Data from the 1988 National Health Interview Survey on Child Health," *Journal of Marriage and the Family 53, Aug. 1991, 573-584*
© 1996 Center for Educational Media

# Why girls need their dads

## "you are worthy to be loved by a man"

Why do girls living with their natural fathers do so much better on average in terms of having lower rates of teen sex and teen pregnancy? The reason probably is that they often receive a powerful message from their committed and present fathers: *you are worthy to be loved by a man, not because of how sexy you look or any other reason, but because you're my daughter. I love you and will always love you.* Feeling secure in their father's love, they are much less likely to seek love from a boyfriend demanding sex. They are more able to stand up for their own long-term interests and wait until they're older to establish love relationships and marriage.

What about father absence and boys? Cross cultural studies by John and Beatrice Whiting at Harvard University found that in cultures where fathers were most absent from the home, more boys grew up to be violent.[22] The same pattern is found in the U.S. Violent juvenile crime parallels the explosion in out-of-wedlock births in the U.S. with a *six-fold* increase from 16,000 arrests in 1960 to 96,000 in 1992, a period in which the total number of young people in the population remained relatively stable.[23]

70% of inmates in long-term prisons did not live with both parents while growing up.[24] David Blankenhorn, President of the *Institute for American Values*, has pointed out that the main predictor of criminal behavior among youth is not race or poverty, it's *father absence. It's boys who don't grow up with their fathers.* Policy analyst Patrick Fagan found that, according to U.S. Census statistics, for each 10% increase in fatherless families, there was a 17 percent average increase in violent juvenile crime.[25]

What do boys often learn from living with their natural father? First of all, they are much more likely to see a daily example of a man who goes to work to support his family, who is committed to the mother of his children. Second, this father is there to affirm on a daily basis: *You're growing up into a young man. You'll do fine. I'm proud of you. I think you're OK.*

Rough-and-tumble play with dad gives boys and girls a sense of confidence and naturalness about their own bodies as well as teaching them how to control aggression when dad says no.

Boys who don't have this ongoing male presence and affirmation are more likely to be insecure about their male identity. They often go to extremes to prove it. They may resist the attempts of their mother to discipline them. Lacking at-home male guidance, they are more likely to carry and use weapons, to join alternative families like gangs, which play by different rules–rules which include the practice of murder, assault, extortion, sexual exploitation, drug dealing and burglary.

Fagan points out that a boy's connection to a caring mother leads to his developing a sense of empathy and concern for the feelings of others. Through his daily contact with a committed father, he gains respect for authority and a sense of discipline, as well as affection and attachment.

The absence of this father/son affirmation can be devastating. Cody Scott, convicted criminal leader of the L.A. Crips, in a July 31, 1994 CBS "60 Minutes" interview spoke bitterly of his hatred of Dick, his absent biological father:

*My mother couldn't protect me and Dick (his father) couldn't–he never came. I hate him. Because I think about where I could have been, you know. And I can't dig that, man, the running out on your kids, you know. The father thing, man.. That's just heavy...because I wouldn't have had to go to the streets to find the street people.*

When his police chief reported rising rates of youth violence, drug use, and gangs, Mayor Bill Hardiman of Kitwood, Michigan decided to speak directly with gang members in his community. He asked them "Is there a father in your home?" Two said they hadn't seen their father in years. A girl gang member said with tears in her eyes, "I've never seen my father."

The gang members explained that they joined because of a need for security and fellowship. They even call the gang a "family." Mayor Hardiman asked, "what can we do to help you?" The girl gang member answered "Clone Cisco (the Youth Director)! He's always there for us, always tries to help us, tells us what not to do, about right and wrong!" In other words, he did *what a father would normally do.*[26]

A National Institute for Mental Health study of families in high-risk, inner city neighborhoods found that: 1) only 6% of children from safe two-parent homes become delinquent; 2) 18% of children from homes that were either unstable or unsafe (broken marriage or lack of supervision) became delinquent; 3) 90% of children from homes rated as *both* unstable and unsafe became delinquent.

The good news is that even in violent and crime-ridden neighborhoods, families with committed, married parents are winning the battle, with 94% of their children avoiding youth violence and delinquency. Most troubled families (broken/absent marriage or lack of supervision) manage to emerge unscathed, with an 82% success rate of their children avoiding delinquency. Their 18% delinquency rate is three times as high as children from intact, safe families, however. Unfortunately, only 10% of children from unstable and unsafe families manage to survive and escape a life of

crime. In other words, children usually avoid a life entangled with the criminal justice system if they have either an absent father or an abusive or neglectful present father, but they nearly always fail to survive both strikes against them without getting involved in crime.

There is so much talk these days about building self-esteem in young people as an antidote to social ills. The truth is that one of the best ways to build self-esteem is to have a *committed natural father in the home.* Just as we must work with all families as they are, whether intact, divorced, stepfamilies or never married to support their natural strengths, we must also help young men and women to understand that strong marriages provide the best and safest environments for their future children to grow up in.

Many young people haven't had either a safe or a stable family. They may have little contact with their fathers or grown up with an alcoholic parent in the home. Whatever their past experiences, don't they want someday to establish a strong, loving, and safe family for their own future children? Ask the average single mother whether she would like her sons or daughters to have a chance to establish a loving and lasting marriage. The answer is obvious.

# Will the 21st Century be an Age of *Relationship Intelligence?*

Barbara Dafoe Whitehead points out that the courtship and marriage system was strongly biased in favor of women in the '50s and '60s. Women had a great deal of control and discretion to accept or reject suitors. Ninety percent of the time first intercourse was closely associated with marriage.

In the new mating system, marriage is not the aim. "Hooking up" is. You have sex on the third date. The goal is to move in together. Men and women go through cycles of hookup and breakup. Sexual intimacy has become connected not to emotional intimacy, but to emotional rejection.

Whitehead is blunt–hookup and breakup disempowers women. Premarital chastity once allowed women to be choosy about their mate when their bargaining powers were at their highest. Women today are pickier about bottle water than about their male sexual partners.

It may be helpful for 20-something women to fastforward to what women in their 30s or 40s experience. Men in their 30s and 40s can marry younger women, but this is not true for most women, despite what movies about romances between glamorous older women and younger studs try to tell us. This gender-biased reality leaves many women hurt and angry. A plethora of books on how to get over getting "dumped" attests to their pain. Many women are realizing that playing the hookup and breakup game while you're young may seem harmless enough, but when you're in your 30s, deeper longrange goals of marriage and children may take on a glaring urgency.

For these and other reasons, as we begin a new millennium, a seachange in attitudes among women about marriage and career goals is taking place. Not all of these women, raised in a "liberated" era when the most important thing was to mind their sexual rights and career opportunities, are happy campers. Many express desires for the kinds of things their mothers held at arms-length 20 or 30 years ago.

Danielle Crittenden, author of the new book, *What Our Mothers Didn't Tell Us: Why Happiness Eludes the Modern Woman*, expresses her mixed feelings in this way:

*Perhaps what is going on is the realization that the progress we've made over the past 30 years hasn't all been net gain. Yes, we are freer than any generation of women in history to hold positions of power in the workplace and in government; but this has come at the expense of power over our personal lives.*

*I've heard many accomplished women complain—without irony—that they don't have the "choices" their own mothers had. Some are college graduates who simply can't figure out how they're going to do it all—or even just one piece of it: Find a decent man to marry, have children and a career, yet also enjoy the sort of family life that was often absent in their own upbringing, as the products of divorced and/or working parents.[27]*

These women have a new problem to face, Crittenden says. Women in the '50s and '60s struggled with the fact that "too many people failed to see that while women were women, they were also human, and were being denied the ability to express and fulfill their potential outside the home." But "today," she writes,

*The problem is that while we recognize that women are human, we have blinded ourselves to the fact that we are also women. If we feel stunted and oppressed when denied the chance to realize our human potential, we suffer every bit as much when cut off from those aspects of life that are distinctly female—whether it's being a wife or raising children or making a home.*

*For if, as women, we were all to sit down and honestly attempt to figure out what sort of lives would make us happy, I suspect that most of our answers would be very similar to one another's, and quite different from men's. They would go something like this:*

*"We want to marry husbands who will love and respect and stay with us; we want children; we want to be good mothers." At the same time, many of us will want to pursue interests outside of our families, interests that will vary from woman to woman, depending on her ambition and talent. Some women will be content with work or involvements that can be squeezed in around their commitments at home; some will want or need to work at a job, either full- or part-time. Others may be more ambitious—they may want to be surgeons or executives, politicians or artists. For them, the competing demands of family and work will*

> *always be difficult to resolve.*
>
> *But I think when we compare our conditions for happiness, most of our lists would share these essentials. The women who don't desire these–those who like living alone or who find perfectly fulfilling the companionship of their friends and cats or whose work eclipses their need for family–may be sincerely happy, but they should not be confused with the average woman.*

••••••••••► Another book, *A Return to Modesty: Discovering the Lost Virtue*, by a 24 year-old writer named Wendy Shalit, challenges the feminist vision of womanhood and charges women's magazines and the mental health industry with seeking to desensitize women to their natural feelings about sex:

*Now it's become pathological, if you have feelings about sex. I see a lot of my friends on Prozac because they think they're too sensitive. And it's just very sad, because we're "curing" precisely the instincts we should be valuing. The women's magazines play a huge normative role [because] they do give advice." "We're all encouraged to become, basically, adulteresses, and grow up to be very sophisticated, hip, "fatal" women. I think the advice is so bad that a lot of women would rather have no advice than to read these magazines.*

Advice from feminists is just as bad, Shalit says, "Feminist author Naomi Wolf says we're all bad girls now, there are no good girls, and we have to liberate our 'shadow slut.' I don't think it's true. I think there are a lot of girls who are good and want to be good, it's just not cool to be good anymore. It's decidedly uncool, because we're all supposed to be jaded and very sophisticated at age 12."

Feminists, Shalit says, now view modesty as "something that we're trying to cure young women of." Sex education, which was supposed to rid women of guilt and shame and build pride in their bodies, and self-esteem in their selves, actually hurts girls–"and boys, too"–Miss Shalit says, by eroding their natural modesty:

*The problem is that we have it so early now, we really don't allow people to develop their personalities before their sexual identity. Every single study" shows that "low self-esteem is correlated with early intercourse for girls. That's very interesting, because we associate modesty with making women weak. That's what we're told—that modesty oppressed women. Then why is the case that women who wait the longest are indeed the ones who have the most self-esteem?"*

*Well, it's because they have a sense of self that is beyond how they view themselves as a sex object. And they want to wait for the right person. There's nothing wrong with that. When you're insecure, you feel like you have to sleep with ... every guy who asks, because otherwise you have 'hang-ups.' You don't have enough self-confidence to say, "I don't have a hang-up. You're just a jerk."*

If girls are supposed to be hip "adulteresses," what does the popular media tell boys? It says: be hard, treat women like b-i-t-c-h-e-s, or female dogs. Even the latest style for boys, baggy pants hanging off the rear end with no belt holding it up, is exactly what prison inmates wear because they aren't allowed to have belts which could be used to cause harm to themselves or others. The "gangsta" style has gone beyond the rap songs, it saturates the clothes many teens wear. If it were just an issue of clothing it wouldn't be so bad. It's the sick, misogynistic attitudes that have the most poisonous impact in communities where marriage is most absent, but also reaches suburban communities like Littleton, Colorado. After all, didn't the two teen killers, Eric Harris and Dylan Klebold, like to shove girls around? When you remove traditional attitudes of respect between the sexes, you often get a regression to a Darwinist survival of the fittest, not "liberation."

If we are to believe the U.S. National Center for Health Statistics, Crittenden's and Shalit's writings seem to express the yearnings of not just a few throwbacks to the Victorian Age, but an emerging trend. Illegitimate births, the driving force of so many other social problems such as child poverty, crime, and school failure, is down. They have tumbled among blacks by 20% in the last seven years and plateaued among whites. And surveys by Yankelovich Partners report that only 37 percent of Americans think premarital sex is acceptable (32 percent of women, 43 percent of men).[28] It's not that the majority of women (and men) want to go back to the 1950s–maybe they are discovering they don't want to be condemned to live forever in the 1960s.

And lest we think that this is a trend only among females, take a look at a study of young urban males by the Urban Institute. The study found that in a hypothetical case of pregnancy involving an unmarried couple, the percentage of males who endorsed having the baby and supporting it rose steadily from 19 percent in 1979 to 59 percent in 1995. The report says these changes, found among whites and minorities alike, are "broadly consistent" with the sexual values reflected in the Promise Keepers rallies and the Million Man March.[29]

The out-of-wedlock birth rate is still distressingly high. For teens it is more than twice as high as Canada or England and 9 times as high as the Netherlands and Japan.[30] The trend, however, is in the right direction. Teens are beginning to see where their true, long-term self-interest lies.

On the college scene, the number of freshmen who say "Sex is OK if both partners like each other," dropped from 52% in 1985 to 42% in 1997.[31] In 1998, a CBS/NY Times poll of 13-17 year-old teens found that 53% of girls and 41% of boys said sex before marriage is "always wrong." The number of high school students who have had sexual intercourse dropped from 55% in 1990 to 48% in 1997. Among suburban girls, ages 15-19, the number who have had sex dropped from 41% in 1988 to 34% in 1995.[32]

Even the rate of divorce is beginning to crack, having dropped from a high of 5.2 per 1,000 Americans in 1980 to 4.0 in 1997, although this is still higher than the rate of 3.5 in 1970 and the rate of other developed countries.[33] In towns and cities with a "Community Marriage Policy" where the churches agree not to marry couples who have not undergone premarital counseling, divorce rates are plummeting. In 16 of these communities, divorces fell by at least 10 times the decline in divorces nationally. In the suburbs of Kansas City, Missouri, where just 40 churches adopted a Community Marriage Convenant, divorces dropped by 35% from 1995 to 1997.[34]

[1] Gloria Steinem may have had personal reasons for having resentment against men since her father was an alcoholic.

[2] Barbara Dafoe Whitehead, "Dan Quayle was right," *Atlantic Monthly*, April, 1993.

[3] Mel Krantzler, *Creative Divorce: A New Opportunity for Personal Growth*, Penguin, 1975.

[4] National Center for Health Statistics.

[5] Ibid.

[6] *Associated Press*, "Marrieds remain majority But percentage continues to decline," January 7, 1999.

[7] 1987 Child Trends survey.

[8] Jennifer Steinhauer, "Study Cites Adult Males for Most Teen-Age Births," *New York Times*, August 2, 1995.

[9] Malas, M.A., "Adult involvement in teenage childbearing and STD," *Lancet*, 1995, 346:64-65.

[10] National Center for Health Statistics.

[11] 1993 *National Kids Count Report*.

[12] Deborah Dawson, "Family Structure and the Children's Health and Well-Being: Data from the 1988 National Interview Survey on Child Health," *Journal of Marriage and the Family 53*, August 1991, 573-84.

[13] U.S. Bureau of the Census, "Poverty in the United States,1992," Series P-60, No. 185, Washington, D.C., U.S. Government Printing Office, September 1993.

[14] Ibid.

[15] Martin Daly and Margo Wilson, "Child Abuse and Other Risks of Not Living with Both Parents," *Ethology and Sociobiology 6*, no. 4, 1985, 197-210.

[16] Judith S. Wallerstein and Sandra Blakeslee, *Second Chances: Men, Women, and Children a Decade after Divorce; who wins, who loses–and why*, Ticknor and Fields, New York, 1989.

[17] Ibid.

[18] Pat Conroy, "Death of a Marriage," *Atlanta Magazine*, Atlanta, GA, November, 1978.

[19] Barbara Dafoe Whitehead, *The Divorce Culture*, Random House, New York, 1996, 100.

[20] Deborah Dawson, "Family Structure and Children's Health and Well-Being: Data from the 1988 National Health Interview Survey on Child Health," *Journal of Marriage and the Family 53*, August 1991, 573-84.

[21] Robert Flewelling, et al., "Family Structure as a Predictor of Initial Substance Abuse and Sexual Intercourse in Early Adolescence," *Journal of Marriage and the Family 52*, February 1990, 171-81.

[22] Beatrice and John Whiting, *Children of Six Cultures: a Psycho-Cultural Analysis*, Harvard University Press, Cambridge, MA, 1975.

[23] "Marriage in America: a Report to the Nation," *Council on Families in America sponsored by the Institute for American Values*, New York, March, 1995.

[24] Bureau of Justice Statistics, *Survey of Youth in Custody,* 1987, U.S. Department of Justice, Washington, D.C., 1988, 1.

[25] Patrick Fagan, "The Real Root Causes of Violent Crime: the Breakdown of Marriage, Family, and Community," Washington, D.C.: *Heritage Foundation Backgrounder,* March, 17, 1995, 23.

[26] Speech by Mayor Bill Hardiman at *Smart Marriages* conference sponsored by the Coalition for Marriage, Family, and Couples Education, Washington, D.C., July 9, 1998.

[27] Danielle Crittenden, "The Next Advance for Women: Early Marriage and Parenthood," January 1999, *The Woman's Quarterly,* Arlington, VA.

[28] John Leo, "The joy of sexual values," *U.S. News & World Report,* March 11, 1999.

[29] John Leo, op cit.

[30] Congressional Quarterly *Researcher,* 1998, 581.

[31] *The American Freshman,* UCLA, as discussed by Karl Zinsmeister, Stephen Moore, Karlyn Bowman, "Is America Turning a Corner?," *The American Enterprise,* January/February 1999.

[32] U.S. National Center for Health Statistics, U.S. Centers for Disease Control.

[33] U.S. National Center for Health Statistics as discussed by Karl Zinsmeister, Stephen Moore, Karlyn Bowman, "Is America Turning a Corner?,"*The American Enterprise,* January/February 1999.

[34] January 1999 *Marriage Savers* Newsletter, 9311 Harrington Drive, Potomac, MD 20854.

# chapter six

# What is your Price Tag?

Rob, a fourth year student at Penn State, loved bike riding in the paths near campus which went for miles and miles. He'd worked several part jobs in order to save up the thousand dollars needed to buy the new titanium mountain bike that was hanging in the window of the bike shop just off-campus. Nearly every day last year he'd gone to look at the bike.

Finally, he had enough to buy the bike. From that day on, he spent many hours riding the bike, in sun or rain, and sometimes even storm. He became one of the best cyclists in the area. His bike was like a best friend, that he took with him everywhere he went. The hours when he wasn't riding the bike he spent taking care of it. He bought brand new tires for it as well.

Soon he would graduate. He'd been accepted at NYU in a graduate program and realized that his mountain bike riding days

were numbered. Not much mountain biking in the streets of the Big Apple. He already had a "city bike" picked out. It was then that Rob decided to sell his bike and told his roommates and other acquaintances that it was for sale. He told them that he might be willing to sell it for $400.

Rich, a junior who lived in the dorm next door ran into Rob the next day and said, "I heard you're selling your mountain bike for $400."

Rob said, "that's true."

Rich said, "well, I've got $200 in my pocket right now. It's yours if you'll let the bike go for $200."

Rob said, "no way. I just put new tires on it."

Rich said, "but it's got scratches on it."

Rob said, "every mountain bike has some scratches. This isn't a bike for riding down the sidewalk in front of your house. It's a mountain bike."

Rich said, "I'll have to touch up the scratches on it."

Rob said, "You don't know how many hours I put into taking care of this bike!"

Rich said, "Look, if you'll change the price, I'll take the bike off your hands."

"You've convinced me. The price is changed," Rob said with a smile.

"Great, here's your $200," Rich said, taking the money out of his pocket.

"Sorry, Rich, the price is changed, but not to $200. The price is now $800. That's $400 less than what I paid for it and that's what it's worth."

"You can't do that!" Rich protested.

"It's my bike. I can sell it for whatever I want. This bike has special alloys in it. This bike won several races. It has new tires. $800 is cheap."

Rich said with a smile, "Look, you're a good salesman. OK, I'll give you $400 for it. You convinced me."

Rob countered, "I mean what I said. This bike is worth more than $400. The more I talked with you the more I realized how much I love this bike. $800 is a bargain, take it or leave it!"

Rich protested and grumbled for a long time, but by the end of the week, he paid the $800 and knew it was worth it.

Rick Stedman, author of a book called *Pure Joy*, tells a story similar to the one above to many single men and women he's counseled to help them think about the way they relate to others and their own sense of value. People tend to treat us the way we let them. The way we let others treat us reflects how much value we put on ourselves.[1]

There are many analogies between sexuality and money. The truth is that sexuality, like anything else that people find desirable, can be treated like a commodity, something that can be used to get what you want. The mass culture tends to promote this point of view. The media keeps on telling us that a girl who is pretty or sexually attractive can get what she wants.

If a girl gets involved in sexual dating relationships, she may, indeed, find that guys are very interested to take her out on dates, but are they really interested in her or as someone to have sex with? Sex can make her powerful and desirable in the short term, and she may think that she is in control, but it can distort the relationships and even herself in a way that may not become clear until later.

Many young people buy into this approach, but find out that the sexual marketplace can become pretty empty after a while. The sex drive is not just arousal-oriented, as some would have you believe; it is *person-oriented*. Sexual release per se is not fulfilling ultimately.

If love and real commitment aren't there, the sex act feels empty. The purpose of sex is not just pleasure, as many people think, it's to communicate value. Just as you don't lend a thousand dollar bicycle to a stranger or someone you don't know well, you don't want to lend the precious gift of your sexuality to someone who may just use and throw it away like a worthless piece of trash.

In Rick Stedman's story, the object being sold is not a mountain bike, it's an old antique table that was on sale for $300, but its owner decides that it's more valuable than that. She demands $600 for it and gets it instead of letting it go for less. After he tells them the story, many single adults realize that it is their view of themselves that determines how others will treat them. At that point, he asks them, "if you were a table, how much would you be worth? Would you be a $300 table, a $400 table, or a $600 table?"

Some say, "I feel like a $10 table. I have given myself away so cheaply and have been treated so poorly that I feel worthless." Others say, "I guess about $300. I'm not going to end up in a thrift store, but I will never receive full price either. I will never be treated the way I would like to be." Still others smile and say, "I'm a $600 table, and I have been waiting a long time for someone to discover and treat me like that."[2]

People won't usually treat us poorly because they view us as cheap. It may be a surprise, but the way others treat us is often a product of our own choosing. If we do not value ourselves, we will probably allow others to treat us poorly. On the other hand, if we truly value ourselves, we will not settle for poor treatment. The "prices" others will pay for us are not set by others—we fill in the price tags ourselves.

What can you do if you feel your price tag would fit in better at a garage sale than at a high-end store? You probably should put other dating relationships on hold until you can find out why you have a "garage sale" view of yourself. You need to grieve for the loss of your sense of value, begin to heal yourself and to reclaim your worth as a unique human being with infinite value.

David Steele founded an organization called *Life Partner Quest* after years of marriage counseling. He realized that the issues that often break couples up are easily identified prior to their making a commitment. Unfortunately, people tend to minimize these issues or to be unaware of them.[3]

Steele identifies several traps that singles may fall into:

1) **Fairy Tale trap.** Trap popular with some women who wait for a Prince Charming to fill their empty lives and to fulfill their every emotional need.

2) **Date to Mate trap.** These women or men are ready to enter into serious commitment after the first date.

3) **Attraction trap.** These men or women are ruled by hormones. If they find someone who is sexually attractive then the case is closed. No more questions need to be asked. But, as was pointed out in chapter two, your hormones are designed to ensure that you reproduce, but are not particularly good judges of whether someone would make a good life-long partner.

4) **"Love conquers all" trap.** These singles interpret infatuation,

attraction, the need for good sex and for attachment as love. "Love conquers all." Need becomes necessity.

Steele points out that happiness has become a need. We need to be happy but don't know how. We constantly try to "get" instead of to "give". We are constantly busy "doing" instead of "being." He speaks from experience. His first marriage failed and he is working on making his second marriage more of a success.

**5) Rescue trap.** Similar to the Fairy Tale trap. These singles are always hoping that a relationship will solve their emotional and financial difficulties.

**6) Co-dependent trap.** These singles feel they need to earn love, usually by rescuing others who are willing to be taken care of, but do not seem to be interested in much heavy-lifting themselves.

**7) Entitlement trap.** Believe they deserve to be happy and get what they want in life without effort. May be looking for someone in the co-dependent trap.

**8) Virtual Reality trap.** "What you see is what you get." These are willing to accept everything on face value. They tend to jump into commitments.

**9) Lone Ranger trap.** These singles don't need anyone else's help. Would milk their own cows or goats if they could, too.

Steele's main advice is to "live your vision" Build it and they will come. Be the Chooser, define your Life Purpose. Then develop a support network/community. He identifies ten elements of a successful "Life Partner Quest":

1. Clear vision and life purpose
2. Thoroughly defined requirements and needs
3. Effective relationship plan including strategies for scouting, sorting and screening
4. Take personal responsibility, be the chooser
5. Ready and available for commitment
6. Self-awareness, conscious choices, values
7. Relationship knowledge, experience and skills

8. Community network, support, coaching
9. Live your vision, be a successful single, not desperate
10. Assertiveness- saying 'no' to what you don't want

## Just Follow Feelings?

Some people are relationship junkies. Instead of investing into a single committed relationship, many people spread their affection, hearts and bodies among many different partners. It's like someone who receives a large inheritance or wins the lottery and spends it partying with different friends and acquaintances. As long as he has money, everyone wants to be with him, but when the money is gone, all the "friends" are gone.

On the other hand, if the person invests the inheritance so that it grows into a larger amount he/she may not have a lot of party-seekers hanging around, but people of value will be attracted to that person as someone who has a promising future.

Are you throwing away your precious sexual inheritance on different partners who won't stay for that long? Or are you saving and investing it as something valuable you want to share with a committed lifelong partner? Not trusting people with your self until you have determined that they and the relationship are trustworthy is part of valuing yourself.

Low commitment relationships are like renting something that you'll never own. You get some immediate use or joy out of it, but there's nothing built up that you can call your own. High commitment relationships are like investing something that you will own when the payments are done. You'll be able to enjoy it for your whole life.

Forget about finding the perfect mate who will "make me whole;" the key is to become a complete person with high self-value who will be a good mate for another and who will attract quality friends and others. Stedman points out that "1 x 1 = 1" but "1 x 1/2 = 1/2." Even if an incomplete person finds a whole person, the incomplete person is still incomplete and the relationship is also incomplete.[4]

## "Spotting a potential abuser"

Dear Ann Landers: I would like to suggest to "Average Girl in Every City, USA," that being abused and humiliated by her boyfriend is not "average." I am living in a women's shelter and going through counseling because of my ex-boyfriend's abuse. Like so many other women, I thought if I loved him enough, he would stop acting like that, but it only got worse. I would like to share some of the red flags I failed to see before I finally sought help.
–Brenda in Dallas

Dear Brenda: No one knows the territory as well as someone who has been there. Your "red flags" should be used as guideposts for any woman who is considering a new relationship. Here they are:

- He comes on as a real charmer and loves you instantly.
- He has problems with authority figures.
- He embarrasses you in the presence of others.

- He is very competitive – and he must always win. On the road, he feels other drivers are competing with him.
- He wants your undivided attention at all times and must always be "in charge."
- He has a dual personality – sometimes adult, other times childish.
- His promises and apologies are meaningless.
- He displays jealousy toward your close friends and family members.
- He can't tolerate criticism and is always defending himself and trying to justify unacceptable behavior.
- He has extreme highs and lows – both unpredictable.
- He is rough at times – love pats become more and more painful. Suddenly, you realize he is a serious abuser, and you are a victim.

November 22, 1997 column

[1] Rick Stedman, Pure Joy: the Positive Side of Single Sexuality, Moody Press, Chicago, 1993.

[2] ibid., 31.

[3] Talk by David Steele at *Smart Marriages, Happy Families* conference, July 3, 1999. For more information contact: *LifePartnerQuest*, 4020 Moorpark Ave., Ste. 204, San Jose, CA 95117. Web site: www.lifepartnerquest.com.

[4] Stedman, op cit., 101.

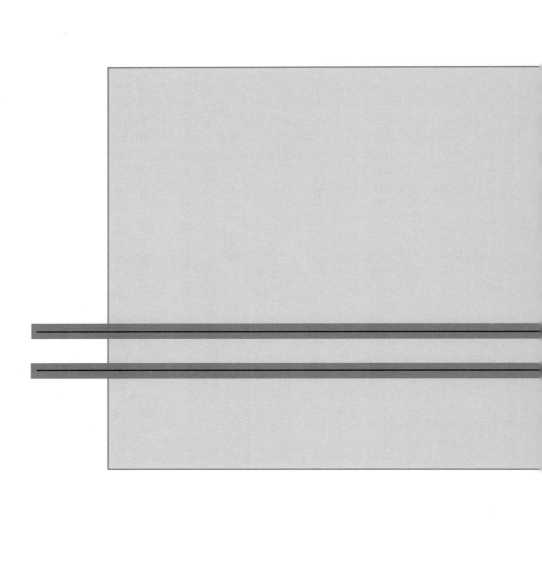

# chapter seven

# TWO cultures

For many years commissions and pundits have warned us that America was in danger of becoming two largely separate societies, one well-off and largely white and the other, poor and largely African-American and Hispanic. It's true that America is in danger of becoming two societies, but the dividing line runs deeper than race or even class. The border is not where most people think it is.

The two cultures are separated by their view of the meaning of sexuality and the man/woman relationship. One culture affirms that the man/woman relationship is a binding covenantal relationship which comes with lifelong obligations and benefits, not just for the children but for the adults themselves. The other culture sees this affirmation as narrow-minded and legalistic and affirms the value of more free-flowing and changing man/woman (or man/man or woman/woman or even adult/child) sexual relationships, but it has failed to explain convincingly how the well-being of children is to be managed, or to acknowledge the high costs of this lifestyle for the tens of millions of child and adult casualties.

And there seem to be defectors from the "no rules" camp. Katie Roiphe, author of *The Morning After* and *Last Night in Paradise*, describes her days in college in this way: "We had the absolute, shimmering freedom that had been dreamed up for us during the '60s. We had the liberating knowledge that no one cared what we did. But it wasn't making us as happy as it was supposed to."[1]

Wendy Shalit speaks of seeing three girls dressed in ultra-

<table>
<tr><td>

**Feminist Pioneer Rejects '90s Sexual Freedom**

</td><td>

Nearly 30 years after her book *The Female Eunuch* hit the headlines, Germaine Greer, the well-known pioneer of modern feminism, now questions where the feminist quest for sexual freedom has led women. Greer says that the strategy of seeking equality with men has led many women to try to imitate their male counterparts, with disastrous results. In her new book, *The Whole Woman*, she paints a gloomy picture of feminist achievements since 1970. For Greer, 60, "to be as competitive, aggressive, lecherous and cruel as men is to be as fragile and miserable as men." Behind the smoke-screen of sexual equality, Greer says, oppression of women continues, making them slaves to men's fantasies and commercial advertising.

Formerly an advocate of sexual freedom, Greer now says that "the constant pressure to be sexually active which has replaced the old pressure to reproduce actually places unmated women in jeopardy, and fills them with anxiety and the sense of failure." Slamming "the notion that people who are not sexually active are of no account", she adds, "let this feminist say it again: no sex is better than bad sex."[2]

</td></tr>
</table>

short skirts on the *Oprah Winfrey* show plead that the "real me is inside." We've succeeded in replacing the housewife ideal with an adulteress ideal, but the new one hides the "real me" as much if not more than the old one did. We've seen an explosion of date rape, because no one knows where the boundaries are so they have to be renegotiated everytime. As proof of growing absurdity, look at the rules instituted a few years ago at Antioch College requiring verbal consent at each stage of intimacy which only goes to show that when you discard old rules new ones that are even more ridiculous are sure to be on the way.

Shalit points to the evolution of language. We've gone from the term "making love" to "having sex" to "hooking up" which sounds like airplanes refueling in the air on their way to somewhere else. It's a myth that modesty = prudery. Promiscuity says "I can't be moved by anything." Sex has no inherent value so I can do it with anyone is the same as sex is dirty so I won't do it at all. Both promiscuity and prudery are based on contempt. Modesty admits, "I can be moved. I am vulnerable because sex is important and meaningful." On MTV, a woman with herpes says "I'm glad I have herpes because now I have a reason to say no to sex." Women feel they have to invent reasons to say no. Since the '60s modesty has become a pathology, a disease, a hangup.

In a song from the 1940s, "Baby, it's cold outside," a young man tries to convince his girlfriend to stay for the night. The girl replies "my father will be waiting for me at the door." Modern feminists would scorn the father waiting for his daughter to come home as just another example of patriarchal oppression, of male control of female sexuality, says Shalit. Now, young women are free to come and go as they wish. They have no support. Then their saying no becomes even more of a personal rejection of the other. So they have to invent excuses or be grateful they have herpes.

A COSMO headline urges "Move from neurotic to erotic." The message is that nonpromiscuous women are neurotic. But the second COSMO headline urges, "Make him commit 100%," oblivious to the blatant contradiction with the first.

Swingers clubs and the sexual excesses of the '60s succeeded in making sex boring. The culture says if you abandon your hopes and innocence then you are mature. In other words to become jaded is to be "adult." But the reality is we have a world of adults who haven't grown up so the kids are forced to grow up too fast.

HELLO CUTIE WHO TIED YOUR TIE?

Women aren't the only ones thinking critically about sexual freedom. Ian Brown, author of *Man, Medium Rare* and clearly a non-traditionalist, fantasizes in a National Republic Radio program about the attractions of an Open Marriage arrangement which would allow him to break the monogamous commitment to his wife. He reluctantly decides to commit to monogamy "for my wife's sake," comparing his decision to foregoing international travel to exotic places like Istanbul. He then confesses to a shift in his own libertarian outlook, "I still want to go to Istanbul, but first I want to go to the small town (representing monogamy) I didn't even know was there." He concludes that "Open Marriage is titillating, but not mysterious. Monogamy is the more mysterious adventure, the last sexual adventure on earth."[3]

Another reason for defections from the no-rules camp is that, at the dawn of the 21st century, what used to be called vice is too much work. The doctrine of "safer sex" was that uncommitted sex is okay as long as you do it "safely." But fear fatigue and a reluctance among the converted to keep using condoms have led to a falling off in their use, so much so that in the summer of 1999 New York University saw fit to host the third annual *National Symposium on Overcoming Barriers to Condom Use*.[4] It used to be that marriage was seen as too much work, too limiting of one's freedom. Now we need national symposia to figure out how to convince people to do the "work" of safer sex.

"The issue is attitude," says Mary Ann Leeper, president of the *Female Health Company*, which manufactures female condoms. "The bottom line is that men and women want to have naked sex, period."[5] It seems a strange argument, but given the utilitarian strain in most Americans, it would seem that more than a few have noticed that the most convenient place to find "safe naked sex" is in marriage.

An article in the Sunday Style Section of the *New York Times* gloomily reports on "Bachelor Parties to Make a Satyr Weep," noting that in New York City, "an aversion to strip clubs is the reason many bridegrooms would prefer their parties to be G-rated rather than G-strung." Philip Baltz, a New York publicity agent, explained why his bachelor dinner didn't take place at somewhere like Billy's Topless: "It (would have) seemed like something out of a bad teenage sex comedy."[6]

Another reason is that in a world without rules, what used to be forbidden no longer contains much mystery. Stacy Morrison, editor-in-chief of *Modern Bride* magazine tells of a bride who gave her husband-to-be vouchers for a strip club. He refused to go. "It's not exactly transgression if your fiancée gives her permission," says Morrison, who notes that "this generation is taking marriage very seriously."[7]

The marriage-affirming culture used to be based largely on the tenets of religion. Indeed, all the major world religions have historically been in agreement about reserving sex for marriage. Of course, religious institutions have been affected in complex ways by a permissive culture. Many pastors are hesitant to speak about the issue. An increasing number of churches, though, have begun to brave the cultural tide by speaking out for saving sex for marriage as part of such programs as "True Love Waits."

In many ways churches have changed significantly by becoming much more open about sexuality. Go to almost any Christian bookstore. You'll be amazed by the number of different books discussing marital sexuality in detail that would never have been tolerated a few decades ago.

A good example of religious enthusiasm for marital sexuality can be seen in the writings of Catholic theologian and novelist, Andrew Greeley. Greeley declares: "It is disgraceful for [God's] followers to mate with each other in any but the most fervent, erotic way. The greater the pleasure that man and woman give to each other–in bed and in every other dimension of their relationship– the more God is present with them."[8] A far cry from the sexual guilt of St. Augustine, indeed!

It is crucial to understand that the marriage-affirming culture

is no longer dependent *solely* on religion. Science, which has often been used to undermine traditional beliefs about marriage, has increasingly become a persuasive supporter.

Scientific research rooted in Darwinism, the ongoing scourge to the Creationist teachings of most religions, now, in effect, affirms the strategic benefits of saving sex for marriage. The evidence that marriage benefits men, women, and children, whatever their race or class, has become very clear. This is not to say that marriages can't be improved. The rigidly authoritarian model of marriage is unlikely to survive in democratic countries. A more egalitarian model is emerging in the U.S. and other countries which will draw even more upon the intelligence, emotional resources and spiritual maturity of couples.

Psychologists like Harville Hendrix are bringing about a sea change in understanding the meaning and, even the necessity, of marriage. Hendrix points out that even health statistics reveal our innate need for relationship. People who are single over long periods of time tend to suffer from depression to one degree or another; they have weakened immune systems and so are more vulnerable to disease and have a shorter life expectancy. Hendrix says it's common for a widowed person to go into decline, to become ill and even die within a year or so of a spouse's death–whether the marriage was a happy one or not.

Those considering a single lifestyle had better consider Hendrix's advice that each of us can begin the process of becoming whole while we are single, but most of us will never wholly heal our wounds or fully recover our wholeness without a partner. In choosing to remain single we are accepting a cap on our development and ignoring the directives of the unconscious at our peril. We are meant to be coupled.[9]

Seen from this perspective, marriage is not the end of freedom, as it is often portrayed. It is often the *beginning of freedom*. It has the potential to be the laboratory for:

*"real healing, deepest intimacy, and the full mirroring of ourselves.*

*When we unconditionally love our partner, making it safe for them to open to love, letting that love sink in over time so that trust can build and allowing their fullness to come back into being, they can begin to feel their oneness. It is the love we give that heals our partner, and it is the love we receive which heals us. It is by loving that we truly change the rigid, brittle parts of ourselves. It is because a committed partnership can bring us back to our original connectedness that marriage is a spiritual path. It is nature's repair process. Through committed couples, nature perfects itself.*"[10]

If marriage is a path of spiritual growth, Hendrix sees divorce as a tragic, and to be avoided, deadend. We get rid of the person and keep the problem instead of getting rid of our problem and keeping the person. We think that a better partner choice and remarriage will solve the problem, but often it's the same drama with new actors.

Our culture has a love/hate relationship with marriage, alternating between adulation and dark cynicism. In the fairy tales, after the prince rescues the princess and the royal wedding, they live happily ever after. If only it were that simple. Learning to love another person takes spiritual maturity. While it's a great disappointment to realize that your "other half" is no longer growing along with you, instead of "jumping ship" or launching a campaign to change his or her bad habits, deepening your own spiritual life is more likely to have a positive and effective impact, at minimum for yourself, and often for your partner.

Fortunately, even divorce is no longer seen as an inevitable outcome. Organizations like *Marriage Savers, Marriage Encounter, Retrouvaille,*[11] and *Divorce Busters* report a 70-80% success rate in saving troubled marriages. Other organizations offer a multitude of programs such as PREPARE/ENRICH and PAIRS to better prepare men and women for marriage or to enrich existing marriages.

Marriage researcher John Gottman says the key to a lasting marriage is something as simple, and profound, as–*friendship.* Successful couples have "a mutual respect for and enjoyment of each other's company." Based on his study of 650 couples tracked for 14 years, Gottman has found that couples who last know each other intimately. They are well versed in each other's likes, dislikes, personality quirks, hopes and dreams. They have an abiding regard for each other and express this fondness in big and little ways, day in and day out.

The quality of their friendship also is the determining factor in whether couples are satisfied with the sex, romance and passion in their marriages, Gottman finds. Successful couples don't let the negative thoughts they have about each other, which all couples have, outweigh the positive ones. And when they do disagree, they make frequent "repair attempts" to fix the damage; their friendship ensures attempts are accepted.

In successful couples, husbands can be influenced by wives, as well as the other way around. That doesn't mean the husband is a "wimp," Gottman says, but rather that there is reciprocity in the relationship.[12]

# What Does Generation Y Think about Marriage?

Probably the best evidence of a trend toward a marriage culture comes from interacting with young men and women themselves. Many children of the baby boomers are experts on their parents' divorces and otherwise complicated lives. They don't want to repeat the same mistakes. The 1999 "State of Our Unions" report by the National Marriage Project found that in a survey of high school seniors, 83% of girls and 73% of boys said having a good marriage and family was "extremely important" to them, but only 64% of the girls and 59% of the boys had confidence that their marriages will last for a lifetime.[13]

Whether they will succeed in their hopes for better domestic lives will depend on many factors. Beliefs or understandings about the significance and importance of marriage will help them see meaning in the sacrifices they decide to make. More than that, they will need to develop relationship skills that were often painfully lacking in their parents' generation. Beliefs, good will, and moral imperatives won't be enough, although they aren't bad places to start.

The realization of a need for relationship skills is leading high school and college students around the country to take courses on the 4th R–relationships. For example, when Marcus Wright, an 18-year-old senior at Martin Luther King High School in Philadelphia, heard his school was offering a relationships class, he knew he had to enroll: "My parents divorced when I was young. So I wanted to find out about marriage because I don't want to make the same mistakes."

Marcus is one of 20 students in the 10-session "Partners" program in which students are joined in mock marriages and told to work through such unromantic tasks as planning a budget, finding an apartment, and writing grocery lists. They also learn about family law issues such as divorce, child support, and spousal abuse. The *Partners* program is taught in 200 schools in 30 states. A similar program, *Connections,* is taught in 350 schools.[14]

Whether these teens are able to achieve their dreams for marital happiness remains to be seen. At least many of them are asking the right questions. Even the Bill and Monica scandal will probably enlighten our culture in the long run, since it was seen and described by friends and foes alike as a tawdry, pathetic affair, not something romantic to aspire to, inspiring pity or contempt, not admiration. On the other hand, the danger is that young people will think that if the President does it and gets away with it relatively unscathed, it's okay.

Let's be honest. There are powerful forces in our culture which benefit from the absence or weakness of marriage. As has been pointed out, these range from financial interests to those who have an ideological bias against marriage, including those who really believe that government programs and social engineering can replace committed fathers, what social historian Francis Fukayama calls "bureaugamy" or the marriage of a single parent to a government bureaucracy.

The vast majority of Americans see the 20th century experiment with sexual freedom as a tragic failure akin to a bad hangover after an alcoholic binge one never wants to repeat again. They yearn for sanity and stability in their relationships. Too bad they've had so few role models. The creators of the mass media often act on their belief that glamorizing dysfunction is more profitable or more cutting-edge than exploring "normalcy."

All it would take to bring about a change of consciousness in our culture would be a few less jaded, more morally-centered media producers. Imagine if the very last show of Seinfeld had featured one of the bed-hopping characters dealing with being infected with the AIDS virus. Wouldn't it be refreshing if reality won out over self-absorption once in a while? A huge opportunity wasted!

Alternative media are cracking through mainstream media censorship/bias against traditional marriage. The enormous

**♥ MY ♥ VALENTINE**

**DIS IS SO ♥ SUDDEN ♥**

popularity of Dr. Laura Schlessinger's nationally syndicated radio program, which is heard by an estimated 18 million listeners, is just one manifestation of the yearning for a traditional, moral, pro-marriage perspective even among people who would not (yet) be considered any of those things in their personal lives. It is mind-boggling how many of the callers to her show dial her 800 number knowing that she will subject them to a verbal inquisition for their infractions of moral law. They make the call anyway. They want to hear a voice of moral authority, one that has been largely missing for more than a generation. Missing no longer.

Marriage involves sacrifices, but they are meaningful sacrifices. Marriage represents the best means we've found yet to give a gift of the love of both parents to one's future offspring. "Alternative kinship arrangements" may look good on paper, but usually leave children falling through the cracks. Our country's future and the well-being of future generations of children are integrally bound up with the health of our marriages. We can have no illusions otherwise.

The cultural divide over marriage mirrors the raging debate inside each one of us. Part of each one of us is attracted to physical or emotional fulfillment separate from life's obligations, leaving others to clean up the mess left behind. This struggle was well represented in the movie, Casablanca. The Ingmar Bergman character is torn between her passionate love for the attractive scoundrel, Rick, played by Humphrey Bogart, and her loyalty to her idealistic, but straightlaced husband, on whom many people's lives depend. Rick pushes his lover to do what is right by supporting her husband, sacrificing his own desires. Such a scene is almost unimaginable today. Too bad, it's our loss.

Most people, deep down, know these things very well. For more and more people the cultural myths which excused short-sighted, self-serving behavior are being demythologized day after day. What looked daring and romantic ten or twenty years ago looks much less so today.

An example of a surprising cultural shift from permissive attitudes comes from, of all places, San Francisco. In that city, for more than four years, the First Offender Prostitution program or "john school" has brought patrons into face-to-face contact with former prostitutes. At one of these sessions, one ex-prostitute shouted, "I hated you!" with so much force even men in the back of the room shuddered. Another said, "I wanted to stick a knife in you!" The men are forced to see a very different side to the women they only saw before as" happy hookers." The San Francisco police say the program is very effective. Of the more than 2,000 men who have taken the class during its four years of existence, only 18 have been rearrested. The program is run together with an aggressive outreach program that helps prostitutes to find an alternative to street life.[15]

Another hopeful effort is the *Institute for Responsible Fatherhood and Family Revitalization* founded by Charles Ballard, now located in Washington, D.C. Ballard, an African-American ex-convict who lacked even a high school diploma, had abandoned his son. After a religious conversion, he adopted the boy, eventually married, and gained not just a high school GED, but a college degree and a Masters in Social Work.

He began working with other men who were not in contact with their children, encouraging them to reestablish relationships, involvement and support for their offspring. Ballard's model has been compared to a "Marriage Peace Corps" since his organization sends married couples into inner-city communities where there aren't many married couples around.

It differs from most government efforts to enforce child support in its goal to reestablish communication and involvement of the father. The group also works in prisons with incarcerated men to encourage them to reconnect to their children even before their release. Ballard says the key to effective change is dealing with men's resentment against their own fathers about being abandoned, neglected, or abused.[16]

# What Can Governments Do?

Given the clear-cut benefits of marriage, one might imagine that government agencies would be supportive of marriage. That is not always the case. Louisiana *has* adopted an optional "covenant marriage" policy which allows couples to choose more rigorous standards for divorce than the "no fault" model used throughout the U.S. where one partner can unilaterally declare a marriage null and void.

A covenant marriage requires a couple to attend pre-marital counseling as well as seek counseling if trouble should arise. Covenant marriages also have specific regulations for separation and divorce. They require an 18-month separation before a divorce is granted. Although covenant marriages emphasize working through problems, they do waive the mandatory separation period in the case of adultery, criminal activity and abuse.[17]

The Florida Marriage Preparation and Preservation Law took effect in 1999. It reduces the marriage license fee for couples who take at least four hours of premarital classes before tying the knot. Couples who don't take them must wait three days to receive their license. The Florida program, which was passed into law through a bipartisan alliance involving Christian Conservatives and Jewish liberals, seeks to inform couples of common problems in marriages and how they can better solve conflicts and improve communication and commitment. The hope, of course, is that fewer couples end up in divorce. Other states are considering implementing laws based on the Florida or Louisianna models.[18]

What about other countries? In Britain, cohabiting couples are almost six times as likely to split up as are those who are married. In Australia and New Zealand the figures are almost identical. Even when there are children, cohabiting couples are five times more likely to have a break-up.

In Sweden, cohabitation is regarded legally and culturally as an accepted alternative to marriage, rather than a transitional or temporary arrangement.This is reflected in the increasing length of cohabitations, and in those who never marry. But despite having the appearance of being equivalent, Swedish cohabiting unions and marriages do not have the same durability. Official studies show that cohabiting couples with one child present are nearly four times more likely to end their union. Data from Norway shows that one in 10 children born to married parents experienced parental separation by the time the child was 10. The same proportion of children of cohabitees did so by the age of two.[19]

In 1998, Paul Boateng, a British Home Office minister, spoke about new government measures to keep parents together and reduce marriage break-ups. The plans include a 15-day "cooling off" period for couples who want to marry in register offices.

Mr Boateng told BBC1's *On the Record* that the Government was not being "preachy" but it could not be neutral about the family: "The family is the building block of society. It's a child's bridge into successful education, it's a child's bridge into good health and development, it's society's first frontline against disorder and crime." He said all the evidence demonstrated that married couples were more likely than others to stay together.[20]

Since the U.S. leads the industrialized world in the problem of divorce and unmarried births, one would expect it to be at the forefront of such efforts. Surprisingly, the *National Center for Health Statistics (NCHS)* no longer monitors how many marriages or divorces there are each year and how this affects our country's well-being. Because of budget cuts, "we had to cut some of the activities within our data collection system," says James Weed of the NCHS. "We couldn't very well cut births and deaths, so we cut marriages and divorces."[21]

According to Michael McManus, founder of Marriage Savers and a syndicated columnist, NCHS used to have five people studying data supplied by the states, but let them all go, and stopped giving $1.2 million to states to collect the data. So California, Texas and Indiana don't even collect the data from counties any more. NCHS used old data from those states in another adjustment to come up with an estimated national number for 1998.

McManus angrily noted, "there are federal employees counting the number of California red-legged frogs and coffin cave mold beetles, two of the 957 'endangered species.' But no one counts divorces. Why not? Ken Keppel, a supervisor at NCHS, said, 'This is the National Center for HEALTH Statistics. *We don't know what the relationship is of marriage and divorce data to health.'*" (*italics added*)

Incredulous that an official at NCHS could be so ignorant of the health correlations of marriage and divorce, McManus cited a book by J.J. Lynch, *The Broken Heart: the Medical Consequences of Loneliness*, which states that:

• a divorced man is twice as likely to die in any given year from heart disease, stroke, hypertension or cancer as a married man.

• death for the divorced is four times more likely via auto accidents and suicide; seven times higher by cirrhosis of the liver and pneumonia; eightfold greater by murder.

• Single women are two to three times as likely to die of all forms of cancer as married women.

McManus also cited Linda Waite's research at the University of Chicago (already discussed in chapter four) which found that:

• a divorced woman aged 48 has only a 65 percent chance to be alive at age 65, but an 85 percent chance to be living if she is married.

• the same 20 point differential exists for men. 83 percent of married men will live to age 65, but only 63 percent of the divorced.

• children of divorce are three times as likely as those from intact families to have a child out of wedlock, and six times more likely to commit suicide.[22]

This was all seemingly new information for the federal Health official McManus interviewed. If the federal government isn't even willing to count marriages and divorces, it will become increasingly difficult to get a clear picture of marital and family trends in our country. Most Americans are somewhat skeptical of politicians wrapping themselves in the flag of "family values," but the truth is that are some concrete things government can do which would actually help strengthen marriage formation, or at least give us a clear picture of the "marital health" of our country. Less rhetoric and more intelligent action would be welcomed by many. A few less taxpayer-funded conferences on arcane sexual practices and a few more conferences on strengthening marriages would also demonstrate a welcome shift in priorities.

On the other hand, as already mentioned, several states have taken leadership in finding ways to promote marriage. Also, the Welfare Reform Act of 1996 did include $50 million per year to fund programs for youth to encourage them to delay sex until marriage and to educate teens about the physical, emotional, and psychological benefits of doing so.

Dianne Sollee, founder of the *Coalition for Marriage, Family and Couples Education,* the organization that sponsors the *Smart Marriages, Happy Families* conferences that take place each year in Washington talks about a marriage *renaissance*. She says that this growing marriage renaissance is based not on a sentimental hunger for more stable families, but on a combination of break-throughs in our scientific understanding of marriage and relation-ships and growing cultural awareness of the need for realistic mar-riage and relationship training. One look at the *Smart Marriages* website (www.smartmarriages.com) reveals an impressive number of marriage education organizations to reduce or prevent marital breakdown before it takes place.

## Marriage in the 21st Century

Will marriages and relationships of the 21st century look exactly like those of previous times? Of course not, but their essence of shared hope will remain much the same. We have the potential to create marriages that are even better than those in the past, although we have to be careful not to stereotype the older "models" as so many have done. It's easier to see the externals than to understand the inner dynamics between two people.

The quality of love we create and grow in our present and future homes will have much more impact on children's lives, than what government does or doesn't do. Thank God. In that sense, the "offices" of father, mother, husband, or wife are just as impor-tant as the office of President, Senator, or Governor, if not more so.

The decision as to how to use our sexual powers is one that each of us must make. The committed model obviously requires a number of sacrifices and considerable self-control. But many are concluding that the benefits outweigh the costs. It is a gift of committed love we give to our children and which they give back a thousand times in their own special, childlike ways.

Success in one's career or other interests can be a real ego boost. But it is the home environment we create together with our mate that will imprint indelible memories, for good or ill, for those impressionable beings we call our children. Investing in them is a profound way for each of us to contribute to our communities and to leave our legacy of love and heart for future generations. Knowing and acting on this fundamental truth is the essence of *Relationship Intelligence.*

[1] Katie Roiphe, "Campus Climate Control," *New York Times*, March 5, 1999.

[2] "Feminist Greer hits the warpath again," AFP, London, March 7, 1999.

[3] "This American Life" WYNC Radio program, February 20, 1999.

[4] Patricia Brown, "The 'Leonardo' of Condoms," *New York Times*, April 11, 1999.

[5] Ibid.

[6] Rick Marin, "Bachelor Parties to Make a Satyr Weep," *New York Times*, April 11, 1999.

[7] Ibid.

[8] Andrew Greeley, *Sexuality Intimacy: Love and Play*, Warner Books, New York, 1988, pp. 178-179

[9] Harville Hendrix, Ph.D., *Keeping the Love You Find: A Guide for Singles*, Simon and Schuster, New York, 1992, 11-16.

[10] Ibid., 47.

[11] Founded in Canada, the name is a French word for "discovery."

[12] Karen Peterson, "Friendship makes marriages a success," *USA TODAY*, April 1, 1999.

[13] "The State of Our Unions 1999," *The National Marriage Project*, Rutgers University, New Brunswick, N.J.

[14] Sara Eckel, "Teaching Teens How to be husbands & wives," *React* Magazine, February 8, 1999.

[15] Evelyn Nieves, "For Patrons of Prostitutes, Remedial Instruction," *New York Times*, March 18, 1999.

[16] Institute for Responsible Fatherhood and Family Revitalization, 1146 19th st., Suite 800, Washington, D.C. 20036. 202-293-4420.

[17] Ashli Sims, "Lawmaker talks on avoiding divorce cycle," 7/19/98.

[18] Associated Press , "State role in premarital counseling is questioned," as published in the *Indianapolis Star*, Sept 15, 1998.

[19] Bruce Logan, "Married parents best for children," *The Press* (New Zealand), February 27, 1999.

[20] Polly Newton, Political Staff, *BBC1's On the Record*, "Straw plans 'put children first," November 2, 1998.

[21] Karen S. Peterson, "U.S. quits gathering marriage statistics," *USA Today*, June 1, 1999.

[22] Michael J. McManus, Ethics & Religion Column #919, "THE NATIONAL CENTER FOR HEALTH STATISTICAL MUSH," April 10, 1999.

# Appendix A: Sexually Transmitted Diseases

In the 1960s, there were only a few STDs to be concerned about, which could usually be cured with a few shots of penicillin. In the 1990s, there are more than two dozen STDs, several of which are incurable viral infections.

Some couples, in order to avoid pregnancy and to preserve the technical virginity of the female partner, practice oral or anal sex. While it's true that there's no risk of pregnancy this way, the risk for STDs is very real, as was found out by a teenage girl who spent weeks in the hospital. Her throat was covered by painful warts caused by the sexually transmitted (and incurable) human papilloma virus (see description below). Oral sex is, most definitely, sex.

Anal sex is even more risky. The sensitive, blood-vessel-rich inner lining of the rectum is easily ruptured and an efficient port of entry for germs to enter the body. Everett Koop, the former Surgeon General, has pointed out that anal sex is a high risk activity for transmission of the AIDS virus and other STDs, whether or not a condom is used.[1] There are also the health risks associated with contact with fecal matter.

• AIDS, or Acquired Immune Deficiency Syndrome, has become the most well-known of diseases which are sexually transmitted and can lead to death because of severe damage to the immune system, the body's defense against disease. AIDS is the last stage of HIV disease which is caused by infection with the Human Immunodeficiency Virus that is known to exist in high concentrations in the blood, semen or vaginal secretions of an infected person. HIV can also be transmitted by sharing hypodermic needles used to inject drugs or by an HIV-infected woman to her newborn baby at the time of birth or through breast-feeding.

It's very important to realize that one cannot tell, just by looking at someone, whether that person is infected or not. The only way to know in the first stage is with an HIV blood test, yet since most tests measure the presence of antibodies the body produces against HIV, the test may not be able to detect infection if someone was infected recently, within the past few weeks or months.

Pregnant women who have any risk factors for infection (such as injecting drug use or sex with someone who does, or multiple sex partners) have been advised to get an HIV test, because treatment during pregnancy of the mother and the infant after birth can reduce the number of babies who develop HIV infection and AIDS by two thirds.

When people enter the last stage of this disease and are said to have AIDS, they develop diseases which are called "opportunistic" because they now have an opportunity to flourish due to a weakened immune system. These can include a type of fungus, viral infection of the eye leading to blindness, rare forms of cancer, damage to the brain, and a rare type of pneumonia. The average time between infection and developing AIDS is ten years. Half of those who develop AIDS die within four years of developing AIDS. 80% die within seven years.[2]

Researchers at the University of Michigan have estimated that during the first 60 days after being HIV-infected, when one could not possibly know that one is infected, HIV may be transmitted to a sexual partner in as many as 3 out of every 10 sexual acts. Infectivity drops as the body's immune system responds, but increases again when one enters the last stage, AIDS.[3]

New treatments including drugs called protease inhibitors offer hope to people with AIDS by reducing the levels of HIV in the blood to extremely low levels. However, these drugs do require a difficult schedule for taking them and often have unpleasant side effects which lead some patients to avoid taking them. In some patients their HIV infection has developed resistance to treatment with those drugs and the protease inhibitors no longer help. Even though very helpful to many, these drug treatments cannot be considered a "cure."

The U.S. Centers for Disease Control and Prevention reports that AIDS is a leading killer of young Americans, claiming a significant number of those who die between the ages of 25 and 44. Many who died in their mid-20s to early-30s were infected as teenagers and twenty-somethings.[4]

Tragic History, Personal Mistakes, Catch Up With A Young Woman Just Beginning to Get Her Life Right.

My daughter, Autumn, always loved the outdoors. She loved sports and any physical activity. She put her whole energy into everything she did. In a way, you could have called her a tomboy in her younger years, but she still had the same kind of hope and desire that all girls share, to someday be in love, to someday be the most special person to a special someone. Autumn didn't have an easy childhood. Her father died when she was two. Her stepfather abused her several times. When I found out what was going on, I was furious and heartbroken at what had happened to my daughter. I felt guilty for having been so blind. We left this deeply troubled, manipulative, abusive man, but the damage had already been done. I tried to reach out to Autumn, but nothing I said, or did, seemed to be enough.

When she became a teenager, Autumn struggled. Her dreams were still important to her, but, partly from not receiving the love of a father and partly from a desire to escape her painful memories, she gravitated toward friends who used alcohol and drugs to get a quick rush of immediate relief.

She struggled with food and weight problems as well as tobacco, alcohol, and drugs. She also engaged in numerous sexual relationships. I tried to get her to stop, but something inside drove her to look for love in all the wrong places.

Autumn wasn't a "bad" kid. She was polite, kind to her four younger brothers, considerate and friendly. But she was terribly confused. She loved her family and we loved her. She wanted to make us happy, but at the same time she felt a desperate need to fill a void in her life. No matter how often she got drunk or high or how many boyfriends she had, the gnawing emptiness never left her. It could only be replaced temporarily with feelings of euphoria which eventually disappeared as soon as the effects of the alcohol, drugs, or sexual experience wore off.

All of us make mistakes in life. Hopefully, we learn from the consequences and learn to find less destructive or risky ways to find happiness and fulfillment. But, my daughter, Autumn, wouldn't get that chance.

Autumn's high school photo

Life went on for Autumn. There were family gatherings and vacations. She finished high school, traveled a little, settled down into a job... had good times and bad. At one point, she thought she might have finally found Mr. Right, a young man named "Alan" whom she fell deeply in love with.

When Autumn was 20 years old, she learned of the death of an old boyfriend. He'd died of AIDS a few months before. Autumn had had sexual relations with him five years earlier when she was 15. I encouraged her to get tested for HIV at that point. The test came back positive. Hoping that it was a false positive, she had a second test done. Positive again.

A feeling of terror and despair gripped my daughter's heart. That night she dreamt that an armed intruder broke into her bedroom, pointed a gun at her face, said, "this is the end of your life," and fired. She woke up in a cold sweat–yesterday couldn't be changed and tomorrow looked like a death sentence.

Unable to face her HIV infection, Autumn fell into denial. Despite our pleas, she hung out with the same friends, went to the same parties, even continued the intimate relationship she had with her boyfriend "Alan," even though this could put him at risk as well. The only difference was that now she carried a secret that no one else knew.

Soon after, "Alan" and Autumn ended their relationship. Fortunately, it seems that he did not become infected. Autumn became more free to focus on her own spiritual growth and development and was able to forgive all the hurt she had received, and given, in the past. She grew a lot in that year and we became much closer, but eventually the disease caught up with her. At age 23 she began experiencing respiratory problems which developed into pneumonia. For the next two years her health continued to deteriorate.

She tried many healing methods, both conventional and alternative. And while most of her days were marked by pain which at times became excruciating, Autumn did experience some periods of

Autumn at twenty-five, just before she died

relief. During one of the good times, she took a trip to Hawaii paid for by friends of the family. Autumn was so inspired by the beauty of the islands, she wrote a poem which I will always keep. In her poem she wrote "I release the past in one final bow...I forgive the one who caused me pain; I forgive myself for feeling shame; I have no need for these emotions; I give them freely in my devotion."

Less than two months after she returned from Hawaii, spinal meningitis, which had been kept at bay with strong drugs and medications returned with a vengeance, more consuming than ever before. Autumn's brain was so swelled and inflamed that the pain was unbearable. No medication could combat that level of agony. She experienced seizures and blackouts. Her vision suffered. Sometimes she could hardly see.

She was admitted into the hospital for the fourth and final time. She never believed that she would die. Which 25 year-old wants to imagine her own death? She didn't talk about it, only about getting better and going home. In spite of her constant pain she tried to be bright and cheerful to all of us around her.

Finally, her brain had one seizure too many. Her depleted body could take no more. Her heart and breathing stopped... emergency measures were taken. She was put on life support. Family members were called to the hospital.

Autumn never regained consciousness. She died two days later. She was 25 years old. Her life was full of anguish, some of which she brought on herself, but also full of hope, joy and a desire for love. In the end she made peace with her past. Those of us who knew her will always love her, aware that she is never far away, even now.

Adapted account by her mother, Taffy Brandt, May 1997

Sexually transmitted diseases which are much more widespread in the U.S. than is AIDS include:

- **Genital Herpes** is an incurable viral infection which:
- infects more than 1 in 5 adults in the U.S. and tens of millions around the world.
- causes open sores or blisters in the genital area which can cause sexual intercourse to become very painful.
- causes pregnant women who have an active case of genital herpes to have surgical (Caesarian) delivery to avoid infection of the baby, which can lead to blindness, brain damage or even death.

• has no cure, although usually it can be controlled with medication. Once you have it, you have it for life.[5]

Here is what some who experienced genital herpes had to say: "my first attack was so agonizing that I had to take two weeks sick leave... and handfuls of pain killers." "Herpes has cost me thousands of dollars, the loss of two wives, and children... It has effectively destroyed my life. I no longer even bother with relationships at all;" "I feel loathsome, worthless and untouchable as a sexual partner."[6]

• **Gonorrhea** is one of the oldest infectious diseases with millions of cases worldwide each year and 1.4 million in the U.S. alone. Sometimes referred to as the clap, it often causes:

• burning, itching, or unusual discharge in the genital area, but may have no or few symptoms, particularly in women.

• Although it can be effectively treated with antibiotics, if not noticed and treated in a woman, it can spread to and damage her reproductive organs.

• Millions of cases of PID, Pelvic Inflammatory Disease, caused by gonorrhea are treated each year. PID leads to sterility in more than 100,000 women each year.[7]

• The infection rates for gonorrhea in the U.S. are highest for sexually active women between the ages of 15-24. [8]

• **Chlamydia** is a sexually transmitted infection caused by a bacterium, Chlamydia trachomatis. Annually, more than 4 million Americans are infected, most of them sexually active adolescents and young adults.

•Symptoms. Most men with chlamydia have a burning sensation while urinating or a discharge from the penis; they may have tender or swollen testicles; some men have no symptoms.

Most women with chlamydia have no symptoms. A minority have a burningsensation while urinating or a vaginal discharge. Women in whom the infection spreads to the uterus and fallopian tubes sometimes have lower abdominal pain, nausea or fever.

• Who's at risk: Teenagers and people in their early twenties are at highest risk because the bacteria can more easily infect their still maturing reproductive organs. The more sexual partners a person has had, the greater the risk of chlamydia.

• If not noticed and treated with tetracycline or other

antibiotics, it can also cause severe tubal damage and sterility.

• Medical Complications: In women, chlamydia can lead to infection of the uterus and fallopian tubes (pelvic inflammatory disease). Scarring of fallopian tubes by chlamydia frequently causes infertility and also increases the risk of a dangerous ectopic pregnancy (pregnancy outside the uterus).

Women infected during pregnancy may deliver prematurely or may spread chlamydia to their infants, causing eye infection or pneumonia. In men, infection sometimes spreads to the epididymis (a tube that carries sperm from the testicle), causing pain and fever.

• Diagnosis: New urine tests available at a doctor's office or health clinicare more convenient and more accurate than cultures and other methods. These tests detect tiny amounts of genetic material (DNA or RNA) from chlamydia bacteria. They can also be used to test a discharge from a woman's cervix.[9]

• In having sex with a Chlamydia-infected partner, one has a 50% chance of infection through each encounter.[10]

• **Syphilis,** which infects 130,000 people each year in the U.S.,[11] is probably the best known STD. One has a:

• one in three chance of infection through sexual intercourse with an infected person.

• causes genital lesions known as chancre sores and rashes on the palms and feet within six weeks of infection. The sores, although painful, heal by themselves.

• can usually be cured with penicillin or other antibiotics. If treatment is neglected, however, the infection advances and eventually can invade the heart, eyes, brain, and other organs, leading to paralysis, blindness, and eventually, death. (Getting treated is obviously very important!)

• An infected pregnant woman can pass it on to her unborn baby, causing meningitis, deformities, or stillbirth.[12]

• **Human papilloma virus (HPV),** also called condyloma, is another viral STD, which

• causes genital warts. Infects 1 million per year in the U.S.

• can lead to cervical cancer. Each year nearly 500,000 women world wide develop cancer of the cervix caused by HPV with an estimated 150,000 deaths.[13]

• girls who have sex as teenagers have an 800% higher rate of cervical cancer when they become older. The cells in the cervix, which is the opening to the uterus, are still developing and more sensitive to infection in teenage women than in older women. Waiting just a few years to have sex greatly reduces their risk for this deadly disease.

• removing genital warts can be difficult and timeconsuming. Treatments include the use of acid, freezing, surgery, electric cauterization, and the use of lasers. Even after removal, patients may find that the warts come back, necessitating further efforts at removal.[14]

• **Hepatitis B** is a blood borne disease which is:

• spread through sex or sharing needles with someone infected and from mother to newborn child.

• infecting more than 200 hundred million currently around the world. There are high rates of infection in China, Taiwan, Southeast Asia, sub-Saharan Africa, Oceania, and the Mediterranean region.

• the most common cause of liver cancer which is very deadly and difficult to treat, leading to the deaths of 1 to 2 million around the world each year.[15]

Which age group has the greatest number of cases of STDs? The answer in the U.S. is 16 to 24 year-olds. This group is infected with more than half of the estimated 12-15 million infections each year in the U.S.[16] Because of the open sores and stress on the body's health caused by many STDs, the danger of HIV infection and quick progression to AIDS are greatly increased by being infected with an STD.

[1] C. Everett Koop, "Victims carry stigma of 'improper behavior'" *USA Today,* September 18, 1987, 13.

[2] HIV/AIDS Surveillance Report, Vol. 9, No. 2, December 1997, Table 13

[3] *Associated Press,* January 6, 1995, "HIV Carriers are highly contagious in first days," reporting on article by John Jasquez in November 1994 *Journal of Acquired Immune Deficiency Syndrome.*

[4] *Associated Press,* "Safer driving cited in rise of AIDS as a top killer," February 4, 1995.

[5] Robert L. Murphy, M.D., "Sexually Transmitted Diseases," *The Biological and Clinical Basis of Infectious Diseases,* 4th edition, W.B. Saunders Company, Philadelphia, 1992, 253.

[6] Charles T. Gregg, *A Virus of Love,* Charles Scribner's Sons, New York,

1983, 251.

[7] Robert L. Murphy, M.D. op cit., 258.

[8] Ibid. Also, *Associated Press*, "Higher Gonorrhea rates among teenage girls," August 20, 1993.

[9] Tomoko Hosaka, "More testing recommended for Chlamydia," *The Washington Post*, August 18, 1998.

[10] Robert L. Murphy, M.D., op cit. 263.

[11] Geoffrey Cowley, et al., "Sleeping with the Enemy," *Newsweek*, December 9, 1991.

[12] Robert L. Murphy, M.D., op cit., 240-252.

[13] Alex Ferenczy, M.D., "Symposium: HPV DNA: quicker ways to discern viral type s, *Contemporary OB/GYN*, 33:4, April 1989.

[14] Robert L. Murphy, M.D., op cit., 264.

[15] Stanford T. Shulman, M.D., "Viral Hepatitis," *The Biological Clinical Basis of Infectious Diseases*, 4th edition, W.B. Saunders Company, Philadelphia, 1992.

[16] Geoffrey Cowley, op cit.

# Appendix B: How Safe is "Safer Sex?"

One approach that you hear a lot about is the practice of so-called "safe(r) sex" which is defined as the consistent, proper use of a latex condom every time you have sex. But how safe is "safe(r) sex"? How much protection do condoms provide?

# Condom Effectiveness and Pregnancy

Studies from the Guttmacher Institute have shown that condoms have a use failure rate of 10-15%, which means that in real practice they failed to prevent pregnancy in 1 in 10 to 1 in 7 married couples who used them to avoid pregnancy over the course of a year.[1, 2] One study indicated that condoms broke during use or slipped off during withdrawal 15% of the time.[3]

The average use failure rate for teenage couples using condoms to prevent pregnancy is 18.4%.[4] That means that in one of five teen couples using condoms, there will be a pregnancy within one year. In two years, one in three teen couples using condoms will have a pregnancy.

Among some teenagers the yearly condom failure rates for pregnancy were nearly 3 in 10.[5]  It is well established that condoms are one of the least effective forms of birth control. Other contraceptives are more effective but provide no protection against infection with sexually transmitted diseases.

# Condom Effectiveness and STDs

Condom failure associated with transmission of STDs (sexually transmitted diseases) could be somewhat higher than for pregnancy for two reasons:

1) only women can become pregnant, whereas STDs can infect both sexes,

2) women are fertile a few days each month, but a person having sex with a person infected with an STD can be infected any day of the month.

While correct, consistent condom use can significantly reduce infection with many STDs, the unfortunate reality is that their actual effectiveness during actual use may be less than most people imagine. Health professionals at a Rutgers University health clinic found no difference in Chlamydial infections between students who used condoms and those who didn't.[6]

Many physicians warn that condom use is of limited use in preventing HPV infection, which you'll remember can lead to genital warts and cervical cancer. The reason is that some sexually transmitted diseases can be spread by skin to skin and skin to sore contact, not just in the area protected by the condom but throughout the genital regions of the two partners.[7] [8]

To summarize, while proper condom use can reduce transmission of certain STDs, it is of limited effectiveness with others. Also, many people exhibit a great deal of carelessness in the use of condoms, carelessness they may bitterly regret in years to come. All in all, for many couples condom use is not insurance against being infected with several STDs.

# Condom Effectiveness and HIV

Studies of condom effectiveness in preventing the spread of HIV show significant failure rates. One well-known study found a 1 in 6 failure rate in preventing transmission of the HIV virus in couples where one partner was already infected who said they used condoms every time they had sex.[9] A study published in 1995 at the Johns Hopkins School of Public Health reported about 204 HIV-infected men who were told to use condoms to protect their female partners, who were not infected. During a 17 month period, among 31 of the couples who said they always used condoms, one in four (23%) of the women became HIV-infected. Among those couples who used condoms sometimes, more than one in three (36%) became infected. Among those who never or seldom used condoms, half (53% and 48%) became infected.[10] Of course, none of those who refrained from sexual contact became infected.

We can see that consistent condom use reduced the infection rate by half, from roughly one in two of those who seldom or never used condoms being infected to one in four of those who always used condoms becoming infected. While this reduction was significant, it was nowhere near total protection.

If someone were offering you free plane tickets to a vacation resort, with all expenses paid, but said that one of the four planes flying may have a bomb on it, would you get on any of the planes? Therefore, the question becomes: how much risk are you willing to tolerate for a fatal disease for which there is still no cure and no vaccine? Other studies show different condom failure rates, so what if the risk is "only" one in ten or one in twenty?

Do condoms reduce risk of infection with HIV and some other STDs? Yes. Do they eliminate risk? No. Is the use of condoms safer than abstinence or mutual life-long fidelity to one uninfected person? The answer is no.

Remember, there are documented cases of people who *were* infected with HIV or other STDs, the first and only time they had sex with the person who infected them. The sex surveys mentioned earlier tell us that married people have the best sex. If they are truly faithful to each other, they also have the safest.

[1] J.D. Sherris, D. Lewison, and G. Fox, "Update on Condoms–Products, Protection, Promotion," Population Reports, series H, No. 6, 1982; R. A. Hatcher, et al., Contraceptive Technology, 1986-87, Irvington Publishers, New York, 1986.

[2] Centers for Disease Control and Prevention, MMWR, March 11, 1988.

[3] J. Trussell, D. Warner, R. Hatcher, "Condom Slippage and Breakage Rates," Family Planning Perspectives, Volume 24, No. 1, January-February 1992, pp. 20-23.

[4] Mark D. Hayward, et al, "Contraceptive Failure in the U.S.: Estimates from the 1982 National Survey of Family Growth," Family Planning Perspectives 18:5, Sept./Oct. 1986.

[5] Elise S. Jones, et al., "Contraceptive Failure Rates Based on the 1988 NSFG," Family Planning Perspectives, Volume 24, No. 1, January-February 1992, pp. 12-15.

[6] S. Samuels, "Epidemic among America's Young," Medical Aspects of Human Sexuality 23:12, December 1989, 16.

[7] John V. Dervin, M.D., "Condom Won't Prevent Transmission of Human Papillomavirus," Family Planning News, 22:12, June 1992.

[8] Mitchell Greenburg, M.D., OB/GYN News, 28:15, 1993.

[9] M.A. Fischl et al., "Heterosexual Transmission of HIV, Relationship of Sexual Practices to Seroconversion," Abstracts from the Third International Conference on AIDS, June 1-5, 1987, Washington, D.C., p. 178. For an overview of amount of risk reduction provided through condom use, refer to Susan Weller's article, "A Meta-Analysis of Condom Effectiveness in Reducing Sexually Transmitted HIV," Social Science and Medicine, Volume 36, No. 12, pp. 1635-1644, 1993, Pergamon Press, LTD, Great Britain.

[10] Mark D.C. Guimareaes, et al., Rio de Janeiro Heterosexual Study Group, "HIV Infection among Female Partners of Seropositive Men in Brazil," American Journal of Epidemiology, Johns Hopkins University School of Public Health, Vol. 142, No. 5, 1995.